THE COSMIC REVELATION:
The Hindu Way To God

THE COSMIC REVELATION: The Hindu Way To God

Bede Griffiths

Templegate Publishers/Springfield, Illinois

Published by
Templegate Publishers
302 East Adams
Springfield, Illinois 62701

ISBN 0-87243-119-3

TABLE OF CONTENTS

PREFACE

These talks were originally given to a mixed gathering at Conception Abbey, Missouri. The talks were taped and then transcribed, but the transcription was very imperfect, and it is entirely owing to the patience and persévérance of Brother John that they have now been given a presentable form. We worked together on them during his long stay in our ashram and I am deeply grateful to him for his help and encouragement, especially as this was given during the time when he was engaged writing an account of his own wanderings as a Christian sannyasi without money through North and South America to India and the Far East. This book is a record, therefore, of our shared enthusiasm for the meeting of East and West in a new vision of life. I have retained the rather free style in which the talks were originally given, and would emphasize that they are intended as nothing more than a popular introduction to the Vedic tradition for those who have no previous knowledge of it.

The Hindu Way to God — The Vedic Revelation

We are going to reflect on what I call the Vedic Revelation; and I use the word revelation intentionally because I think we have to recognize today that God has revealed Himself in other ways than through the Bible. God has been speaking to man, "in many and various ways," as it says in the letter to the Hebrews, from the beginning of time.

Today we are aware of the presence in other religions of a wisdom and experience of God which challenges the Church. I feel that we are really entering a new epoch. For almost two thousand years the Christian Church grew up with the understanding that it alone was the true religion; that there was no religion outside Christianity which was not fundamentally false, or at best no more than a natural religion. Only today, in these last few years, have Christians begun to discover the riches which God has lavished on other nations. I like to recall an inter-religious meeting that we held in our ashram, at Shantivanam, some years ago where a representative of the Secretariat for Non-Christians in Rome, said: "We come to share one another's spiritual riches."

I believe that this expresses the mind of the Church today. We have come to share one another's spiritual riches. We have the immeasurable riches of Christ to share with others. But today we recognize that God has also lavished his riches on other people. It is a great challenge to our faith and to our

7

religion to relate ourselves now to these other religions.

So when we study the Vedic revelation, the Vedic scriptures, we must approach them as something which God has given to man. There are defects, no doubt, in every scripture where God and man work together, but there is something of the "word" of God in the Vedas. They speak of *vac*, the Sanskrit for 'word,' in the Vedas as the mediator between God and man. Therefore I would like to approach this subject in a spirit of reverence and of humility and with a great desire for truth. And where there is anything challenging, let it be tested by whether it is true to Christ and to what God has revealed in Christ, and let us try to see other religions in their relation to him.

In India we often begin talks with the Gayatri mantra, a short chant. It is the most sacred mantra of the Vedas, and is used again and again as the most sacred utterance. It may not seem much at first, but the more one reflects on it, the more meaning it has.

> *Om bhur bhuvah svaha*
> *tat savitur varenyam*
> *bhargo devasya dhimahi*
> *dhiyoyonah pracodayat*
> *om shanti shanti shanti*

The translation is: 'Let us meditate on the glorious splendour of the divine light. May he illuminate our meditation.' The chant is preceded by the word *Om* which is repeated three times. It is a sacred word; like *Amen* from the Hebrew. And we end with *shanti, shanti, shanti,* 'peace, peace, peace.' This is the peace of God which we invoke on ourselves and on the whole world.

In this spirit of reverence we approach these Vedic Scriptures. The word *veda* means 'knowledge,' the same as the Latin root *video* to know, to see. The Vedas are the sacred

8

scriptures of India and the consensus is that they date in their present form from about 1500 B.C. In this form, ancient as it is, they already show a long history of development. The Vedas were written in Sanskrit; and Sanskrit is perhaps the most beautiful and elaborate language in the world. They were brought to India, as far as we know, during the Aryan invasions of the second millenium B.C., which brought the Sanskrit language and the Vedic religion with them.

Veda means 'knowledge,' not simply human knowledge but knowledge that is given by God. The Vedas are called *sruti* from the root *sr*, which means 'to hear.' So the Vedas are what has been heard — not what has been made up, but what has been heard.

The authors of the Vedas are called *rishis*, which some think comes from the root *drs*, 'to see;' they are 'see-ers.' There is no doubt in the mind of the Hindu that these scriptures are a revelation, something which has been heard and seen. They use two other words in describing them. The first is *nitya*, that is, 'eternal.' Most ancient religious traditions will say that their scriptures are eternal — the Torah of the Jews, for instance. The Jews always say that the Torah is eternal and that God revealed it to Moses. So also the Koran is said to have been written on tablets in heaven and dictated to Mohammed by the archangel Gabriel. Thus the Vedas also are eternal. Secondly, they are called *apauruseya*, 'without human authorship.' So they are what has been heard, what is eternal and has no human authorship. We are in the presence of what we must surely call a revelation. It is not the same as the Christian revelation; it is in fact different in many ways. I hope that in the course of these talks we will come to understand the differences between the Vedic revelation and the Christian revelation, but I think we have established that it is legitimate to use this word 'revelation' of the Vedas.

The Vedas are a little complex and it is not necessary to

remember all the details, but for those who are interested there are actually four Vedas. The first is the *Rig*-Veda. *Ric* means 'hymn' and this forms the main part of the Vedas. They are hymns addressed to the gods. The Rig-Veda is the most ancient and dominant part of the Vedas. Then comes the *Sama*-Veda, the musical setting for these hymns, which were chanted at the sacrifice. The centre of the whole Vedic religion was the fire sacrifice, of which we will speak later. Thirdly, there is the *Yajur*-Veda, which is the Veda of the ritual formulas of sacrifice. They were written both in prose and verse to be used at the offering of the sacrifice. Finally there is the *Atharva*-Veda, which belongs to a different strata. The Rig, the Sama and the Yajur are the original Vedas. The Atharva-Veda comes largely from the indigenous people, it is supposed, and consists to a very large extent of oracles and charms and magic spells. But it has also some wonderful philosophical and theological doctrine — showing a more developed stage of religion.

The Vedas proper are not of great practical importance today. They are very little read except by scholars. After the four Vedas there are three stages of development of Vedic revelation: the first is the Brahmanas. The Brahmanas are the commentaries on the sacrifice. Very early the sacrifice was thought to be the centre of the whole religion. The sacrifice had a mystical meaning, often a magical meaning. The Brahmanas revealed this mystical meaning of the sacrifice and also all the details of it. They are rather boring to read but they have gems within them.

The Brahmanas were followed by the *Aranyakas*, the 'forest books' — *aranya* is 'forest.' This marks the great turning point in the development of the Hindu religion, in fact in the development of Indian history, or I would even say the history of the world. It was at this point that the seers retired into the forest to meditate. Thus, from being a comparatively external religion, centred on the fire sacrifice, it became an interior religion. They sought to build the fire in the heart. The word *tapas* means 'asceticism, self-control, discipline' — there is no exact translation — but its original meaning was 'heat.' The belief was that when one practiced this self-discipline, this self-control, one generated an inner heat, an inner fire, and so instead of building the fire outside and making offerings to God on it, one built the fire within and offered one's thoughts, one's sins, one's whole being in this interior fire. This is the turning point: interior religion manifests itself, and all the depth of Hindu religion stems from that movement.

The third and final stage is that of the Upanishads, which are the discussions of the seers, the *rishis*, with their disciples. Today very few people read the Vedas, the Brahmanas or the Aranyakas, but the Upanishads are the central teaching of Hinduism. They are the actual inspiration of all that is most authentic in Hinduism, and they are what we ourselves have to study. The word *upanishad* literally means 'to sit near to' and it is supposed to indicate the disciples sitting at the feet of the master. The Upanishads are the discourses of the master to the disciple. They are intended to create and develop a mystical experience. This must be clearly understood, be-cause so many European scholars have been led astray. They approach the Upanishads as if they were the dialogs of Plato, or some philosophical treatise. They miss the mystical mean-ing and consequently misinterpret the main message of the Upanishads. So we have to be cautious of the scholars when we are studying the Upanishads. The Upanishads are often known as Vedanta — the end of the Vedas, the final stage of the Vedas, the quintessence, one could call it, of the Vedas.

To complete this background I would like to suggest some translations. The most important recent work in English is *The Vedic Experience* by Raymund Panikkar. Panikkar has

II

an interesting background. His father was a Hindu, his mother a Spanish Catholic. He was brought up in Spain and studied there first, then in Germany and later in Italy. Finally he came to India. Since then he has divided his time between India and America, where he lectures at Santa Barbara University. For ten years or more he devoted himself to this translation of the important texts of the Vedas, rendered in good English, with notes and commentaries. It is a unique work — rather expensive, but very rewarding. No one before has really opened up the religious meaning of the Vedas in English as he has done.

Secondly, I always recommend the Upanishads in the translation of Juan Mascaro, in the Penguin Classics. This is very cheap and very readable. It is an excellent translation, in good English, though a little free; but he is a good scholar, a professor at Cambridge in Sanskrit. He is reliable on the whole, though he gives a slightly Christian tone to the Upanishads. It is a curious coincidence that the three authors I am going to mention are all Catholics. It shows that Catholics have taken a deep interest in these studies. Mascaro has also done an equally good translation of the Bhagavad-Gita, which is a compendium, one could say, of Vedic wisdom. It does not belong, strictly speaking, to the *sruti*, the revealed scriptures. It is of a slightly later date, but it gathers together the wisdom of the Vedas. If you want to have one book in which the essential teaching and the essential spirit of the ancient Hindu scriptures is to be found, you can find it in the Bhagavad-Gita. It means 'the song of the Lord' — (*bhagavan* means 'the Lord,' *gita* is 'song').

Finally, a more scholarly work is *The Hindu Scriptures* by professor R. C. Zaehner, who was a professor at Oxford. Originally a Zoroastrian scholar, he devoted all the later part of his life to the study of Hinduism. This book was published in the Everyman Library. He gives extracts from both the

Rig-Veda and the Atharva-Veda, some parts of the longer Upanishads and some of the short Upanishads complete, plus the whole of the Bhagavad-Gita. In that one volume one has the essential teaching of the whole Vedic tradition. I must say that his is a scholar's English and I find it unreadable. However, if one wants to come a little closer to the Sanskrit and to what the exact meaning is, one can go to Zaehner.

That is the background. I would like to take it a little further, however, in order to link up the Vedic religion with modern Hinduism. One might easily ask the question: what relation has this Vedic religion along with the Upanishads and the Bhagavad-Gita, to the religion of the Hindu today? I would like to divide Hindu history into periods of a thousand years. It is a very simple and convenient system. The Vedic period is from 1500 B.C. to 500 B.C. The Rig-Veda is about 1500 B.C., the Upanishads, particularly the more ancient classical ones, about 600-500 B.C.

After the Vedic period comes the period of the epics, the *Ithihasas* as they are called: the *Mahabharata* and the *Ramayana*. These are the great popular works of Hinduism, written in very attractive poetry and recited in all the villages, all through the centuries, and dramatized, and more recently also made into films. They comprise the popular religion. They were composed between 500 B.C. and 500 A.D. It actually took hundreds of years for them to achieve their final form. They are a treasury of Hindu wisdom as it accumulated and it is here that modern Hinduism began to evolve.

This is the time when the Aryan invaders came down from the north into the Punjab and then into the Gangetic plain, thence to spread south throughout India. They met the indigenous people of whom the most important are the Dravidians. Where we live, in Tamil Nadu, the Tamil people are generally said to be pure Dravidian, whereas northern India is mainly Aryan, but Hinduism today is a kind of marriage between the northern Aryan religion and the southern Dravidian religion. They are very different: the northern religion is much more a religion of a nomadic people, of warriors, and much more dynamic; the southern religion, the Dravidian, is more a religion of the earth and the Mother goddess. In all the villages around us in South India the principal temple is always that of the Mother, the Mother goddess — she is the object of worship. In those thousand years from 500 B.C. to 500 A.D. these two races and cultures were meeting, and Hinduism evolved from that creative meeting. That is why it is so rich; it combines so many opposites. In this period we also encounter the *Darshanas*. The Darshanas are philosophies. They contain the germs of all the later philosophy. Some of them are not of great interest today, but two forms have continued to develop ever since: Yoga and Vedanta.

In the next period (500-1500 A.D.) Yoga and Vedanta underwent a constant development. Yoga is the practical discipline and Vedanta is the metaphysical doctrine of man's union with God. They constitute the two main schools of Hindu religion.

The period from 500 A.D. to 1500 A.D. corresponds with our Middle Ages. Among the works of this period are the *Puranas*, which followed the epics and are the source-books of Hindu mythology. In this middle period we witness the great flowering of Hindu culture, the building of the great temples with their magnificent architecture and sculpture, the development of popular hymns and songs and literature of every kind, and the growth of music and of dance — all this developed during a great period of religious culture like the Middle Ages in Europe.

From 1500 A.D. to the present day, there was a period of decline and renaissance. It is important to remember that the Hindu religion underwent a gradual decline, very like Christianity. Christianity in the 18th century was at a very low ebb;

it was a period of universal scepticism. Hinduism suffered in a similar way. It seemed to be dying out and all its worst abuses came to light. It was a period of universal decline. Hinduism has its dark side, as every religion has, and it reached its nadir in the 18th century. Then in the 19th century came the Hindu renaissance, and we have always to remember that we are now living in the middle of a Hindu renaissance.

It began with Ram Mohan Roy, a great anglophile, who wanted to combine the wisdom of the Vedas with that of the Gospel. He was deeply impressed with the ethics of the Gospel and visualized a kind of synthesis, which led him to found the *Brahma Samaj*. It was influential for a long time, and many people thought at the beginning of the 19th century that Hinduism would be converted to Christianity. English language and education was being introduced at every level, and there was a strong missionary presence of various denominations. It appeared to be a great opportunity.

But God willed otherwise and when Ramakrishna came, between 1836 and 1886, he renewed Hinduism in all its aspects. He was an almost illiterate Brahmin, yet a man of extraordinary holiness and extraordinary powers. He developed these powers from a very early age and became a great guru. His famous disciple Vivekananda organized an order in his name — the Ramakrishna Mission — which is still strong in the West as well as in India. He made of this neo-Hinduism a force in the world. From this beginning the renaissance has continued. That is why in India today conversion is extremely difficult, if not impossible. In all the Christian colleges and schools, where there are hundreds of thousands of Hindu pupils, scarcely one becomes a Christian; and if anyone does, it arouses very strong feelings. Hindus are very sensitive about conversions. This is very important for our understanding of the situation in India. In their renaissance Hindus are recovering their ancient tradition — studying Sanskrit, reviving the Vedas, popularizing the Upanishads and the Bhagavad-Gita, not to speak of Hindu music and dance. Yoga and Vedanta are being carried over to the West, especially to America, and there are schools of Yoga everywhere today. We are in the midst of that renaissance.

This is the challenge to the Church today. Hinduism is very much a living religion, and Hindus are keenly aware of its depth and its antiquity; they call it the *sanatana dharma*, the 'eternal religion.' They say it has no beginning, that it goes back to the beginning of time, and they are making it known all over the world. That is why I feel that the Church today has been challenged. Christians are challenged to understand this religion, to enter into its inner depth, because it is essentially a mystical religion. It is not a matter merely of rituals and doctrines. If one tries to discuss Hinduism on the level of ritual, though there is a common base in the cosmic revelation, yet if one goes to a Hindu temple one may be completely mystified; it belongs to another world of symbols which are strange and bewildering.

Again if one starts with doctrines the arguments are endless. There are innumerable Hindu doctrines which one can compare with similar Christian doctrines, but it is difficult to reach any agreement. But when one comes to the level of interior experience, that is where the meeting takes place. One of the two founders of our ashram in south India, Father Le Saux, a French Benedictine monk, wrote a book called *Hindu Christian Meeting Point in the Cave of the Heart*. It is in this cave of the heart that the meeting has to take place. That is the challenge. It's no good just studying Hinduism in the university or reading about it in books. We have to live this Hindu experience of God, and we must live it from the depth of our experience of God's revelation in Christ and in the Church. That is the challenge to us today.

Now we come to the doctrine, if I may call it that, of the Vedas. Again, when we use a word like doctrine we have to be very careful. In the West we have developed everything along the lines of doctrine and we consider Christian faith in the light of belief in certain doctrines. But in Hinduism everything turns to experience. It is the aim of the Upanishads to awaken this experience, and it is the aim of every devout Hindu to have this experience of God. What we have to discover is that experience of God which has its roots in the Vedas, which comes to light in the Upanishads and is given its fullest, most perfect expression in the Bhagavad-Gita. I hope in these six talks to cover that ground. It's a great deal, but I want to concentrate on this experience of God as something meaningful and valid for the Christian and for the whole of the world.

I believe that God has given this experience of the Upanishads, the Gita, and the Hindu tradition to the world. We are being called to encounter it and to relate it to the Christian experience of God. In our ashram we have had many people coming to share this experience with us and we have found that those who come with a mature Christian faith find that their faith is enriched and deepened by this experience of the Hindu scriptures. I may say that immature people can be thrown off their balance very easily if they have no deep understanding of their own faith. One must really understand one's Christian faith and live one's Christian faith, and only then can one understand and live out the Hindu experience in the light of Christ. That is the real challenge. It is a particular challenge to the monastic order because our one aim in life is to seek God. We have other works which we do, but the call of a Benedictine monk or nun is essentially to seek God. What the Hindus have been doing from the time of the Vedas to our time is a constant search for God, a search to find out the ultimate truth and ultimate reality, and to experience it in the depth of the heart. That is what we seek.

Now we come to the Vedas themselves and immediately we come up against great problems. Many will say that the Hindu religion is polytheistic and from that point of view dismiss it altogether. The Bible is very emphatically monotheistic, but in the Vedas there are hymns to different gods.

A deeper knowledge makes us realize that the Hindu understood this relationship of the one and the many in a way different from the Hebrew. The Hebrew tradition began with many gods. As you may know one of the words for God in the Hebrew, *Elohim*, is plural. It must have been 'the gods' originally, but in the course of their history the Hebrews learned that this *Elohim* was not many, but one; and his name, as revealed to Moses, is Yahweh. They were forbidden to worship any other god. They recognized other gods at first: as the psalm says, "The Lord, the God of gods, has spoken." In many of the early parts of the Bible they speak of these other gods. But Yahweh was supreme above all the gods. And then, in the Prophets, Yahweh was seen to be everything and the gods of the nations were nothing in comparison. The last stage is that the gods of the nations become demons. So first of all they are "gods," as in the book of Job: when the sons of God appear before God, Satan is among them. Then they become nothing. Finally they become anti-gods: they become demons. This is the tradition which we have inherited and this is why Christian missionaries on the whole have simply rejected Hinduism as polytheism and therefore against God.

The Hindu approach was the exact opposite. We find it defined very clearly in the Rig-Veda itself. In the first book of the Veda, (not first in time; the first in the collection), it says: *"Ekam sat vipra bahuda vadanti"* — "the one being the wise call by many names." The Hindu view is that the gods and goddesses are the names and forms of the One Being who has no name and no form.

This is a very profound doctrine. The ultimate worship of the educated and instructed Hindu is always to that 'one being', the *ekam sat*. The gods are names and forms under which the one God manifests himself. It is interesting to find, as the result of certain surveys recently made show, that even the villager today has the same understanding. They will say quite spontaneously that there is only one God and that the gods are *nama rupa*, names and forms of that one God.

Now that is quite a coherent view. There is one absolute, infinite, transcendent Being who is beyond all the gods and all that can be named in heaven and on earth. The gods are *devas* in Sanskrit, 'the shining ones.' They are much more like the angels, though that distinction was never made clear as in the Hebrew tradition. They are perhaps nearest of all to the "cosmic powers" of St Paul. The gods of the Vedas are the powers of nature, powers of the sky, powers of the earth, powers of the sea, powers of the fire, and our own powers — the power of sight, for example: we look out on this world around us, and that is a divine power. There is a god who is enabling us to see and to hear, to speak and to act. All these are powers of the One Being. That is the basic Hindu understanding. And that is why we must be very careful when we hear words like polytheism being used about Hinduism. It's not really polytheistic. Polytheism is the worship of the many apart from the One, and many Protestants would say on the same grounds that Catholics are polytheists, that they worship the saints. There is probably some truth in that. An ignorant person is always in danger of making an absolute of a particular personal form and worshipping not God in the saint but the saint in himself. But the traditional doctrine is that there is one infinite Being, and all the gods and goddesses and all angels and saints are forms and manifestations of that One. That is our first and fundamental point.

The Cosmic Revelation

I have to go to a deeper aspect of things now. That is: if we are to understand the Vedic revelation, or any ancient religion at all, we have to change our understanding of the world. We have all been brought up in this 20th century world in which we think of matter, as Descartes described it, as an "extended substance." There's something extended outside ourselves. Then we have a mind, and that mind is quite different and distinct from this matter, this world. Science is the process of the mind observing this external world. Then, for those who believe in religion, beyond this matter and beyond this mind there is a God, above everything. That is the three-tiered universe which we have inherited.

It is a well-known fact that modern physics is demolishing this view of matter. Matter is no longer conceived as an extended substance in that way at all. It has been described as "a web of interdependent relations," forming an organic whole. Modern physics itself is changing our idea of the structure of the universe. It is also saying that this physical world cannot be separated from the psyche, from the consciousness. Instead of a separate, extended world and a separate mind we have a field of energy which has its own laws and structures but which is also interdependent with the whole psychological world, the world of consciousness. You cannot separate the world from consciousness anymore. We have a physical world and a psychic world which are interrelated and interdependent.

But, beyond the physical and beyond the psychic is the spiritual world, the world of Spirit, *spiritus* in Latin, *pneuma* in Greek and *atman* in Sanskrit. That Spirit though separate from matter and soul is yet interwoven in the whole structure.

So we have body, soul and Spirit. Now this takes us back to the early Christian concept that man is body, soul and spirit. It is found in St Paul, in the letter to the Thessalonians, and in St Irenaeus and in Origen amongst the early fathers. After that it faded out, but these early Christians had a much more integrated view of humanity. Man is an integrated whole of body, soul and spirit, not a body separated from mind, with God somehow separated from all. I would like to support this with a theory which I discovered about 50 years ago when I was studying English literature and which I have never forgotten. I give it to you for what it is worth, but it changed my whole outlook on life. It came from a book called *Poetic Diction* by Owen Barfield, a friend of my friend C. S. Lewis. He had made a study of words as a literary critic. He took the word "spirit" and pointed out that in most languages that one word *spiritus* can mean wind or air or breath or life or soul or spirit. It has six distinct meanings.

In the first chapter of Genesis one reads in the ordinary translations that "the spirit of God brooded over the waters." But in later translations, in the Anchor Bible for instance, which is very scholarly, it says, "a wind from God brooded over the waters." Now, which is right? What Owen Barfield said was this: in the beginning words contained all of these meanings; they had not been separated out. The word *spiritus* meant wind and air and breath and life and soul and spirit. And then gradually men began to make different words to distinguish the wind from the air, from the breath, and from life. But primitive languages, and Sanskrit is the perfect example, are immensely rich. Often one does not know exactly what a word means, because it can mean many things. This is very relevant for the Vedas, because the Vedas have many prayers for cattle and horses, and for butter and wealth and so on, and the early European commentators always looked on this as a very materialistic religion. But Sri Aurobindo, whom I consider the greatest philosopher of modern India (he died in 1950), in his book on the Vedas made it clear that all these words have a psychological as well as a physical meaning. In certain texts it is absolutely obvious. So that this 'butter' for instance, which comes from the cow, this gleaming butter with all its richness, is also the butter of the mind. The mind produces this butter of thought and the same word can mean butter and thought. The same is true of innumerable other words. Modern critics have begun to discover that the Vedas have this characteristic: every single thing in the universe is understood to have three dimensions. They speak of three worlds. Everything has a physical being and a psychological being and a spiritual being, and it's no good trying to separate them. A very good example is fire. As I said, the whole Vedic religion is centered on the fire sacrifice. The god of fire is *Agni*, and worship was paid to the sun as the source of fire. But the sun is the source of light to the mind as well as to the body. In ancient religion the sun is never merely a chemical body as we think of it, or the moon a physical object from which we can take specimens. The sun and the moon are physical bodies, but they have a psychic dimension and beyond the psychic dimension they have a spiritual dimension. They are manifestations of a supreme spirit. One approaches the sun and the moon and the earth and the trees and the flowers with reverence because God is in the midst of them. We have lost that — they are just specimens to us.

The Western world must recover this ancient vision of the three dimensions of reality. Then everything is sacred. That is what one finds in India; everything is sacred — eating or drinking or taking a bath; in any of the normal events of life there is always a sacred action. When a Hindu takes a bath in the morning he remembers that the water comes down from heaven and it is said to be received on the head of Shiva, the great god, who distributes it through all the rivers of the earth. He receives the water which comes down from heaven and gives thanks to God who sends it down as a sacred river. We have lost that awareness.

Agni, as we have said, is the god of fire. The fire is centred in the sun. You can lift up your eyes to the sun as the source of physical heat and light. That fire comes down from heaven and is buried in the earth and when you take twigs or a flint and rub them together, the fire, Agni, leaps up. This is the god of fire who has come down from heaven to consume the sacrifice. But this fire is also a spiritual fire. There is a beautiful verse in the Rig-Veda addressed to Agni: "O All-knowing One, may your flames that convey oblations to the gods direct our sacrifice." Agni, the fire, is the All-knowing One. It is a physical fire, yet they call it the fire of knowledge, of wisdom, and he is the All-knowing One. He is the mediator between God and man. He takes the sacrifice, consumes the sacrifice and carries it back to heaven, and you ask him to direct your sacrifice. That is one very simple example of this sacramentality of the universe. The whole creation is pervaded by God.

There is another difference between the Hebrew and the Hindu, which I think we need to reflect on. The Hebrew begins always with the transcendence of God. God is infinitely high above the heavens. And God comes down to earth. The whole Christian vision is of God above descending to the prophets, becoming incarnate in Jesus, sending His Spirit, and communicating Himself through the Spirit to all. So it is a movement of descent from above. For the Hindu it is the exact opposite. God is immanent, immanent in every created thing — in the earth, in the water, in the fire, in the air, in the plants, in the animals, in people — everywhere God is present. This is a deeply Christian view, but it has been largely lost today. The Christian tends to think always that God is above. That is why Bishop Robinson was concerned in his *Honest to God* about the God "up there." These are all obvious misunderstandings, but the misunderstanding is due to the emphasis on the infinite transcendence of God and the neglect of His immanence, His presence, in the whole creation. I would like to recall, as an illustration of that, a story told by Father Monchanin, our founder, who was for some years serving as a parish priest in our neighborhood. There was a school attached to the parish, and one day he went up to a group of children and asked them, "Where is God?" Some were Catholics and some were Hindus. All the Catholic children pointed up: God is in Heaven. All the Hindus pointed to their breasts: God is in the heart.

These are two different ways of looking at God: God is everywhere and nowhere, but you can think of Him as above and you can pray to Him and ask His grace to descend, you can kneel in penitence, and ask for mercy. This is obviously a completely valid way. But equally you can think of God as immanent, present in the earth, in the water, in the air. There is a beautiful passage in the Upanishads which says: "To that God who is in the plants, to the God who is in the trees, to the God who is in the earth, to that God who is in everything, adoration to Him, adoration to Him."

I feel these two different ways are complementary. Just as the Christian, starting from above, discovers the Holy Spirit as immanent and realizes the presence of God in the whole creation around him, so the Hindu, starting with the immanence of God in the creation, in the human heart, rises to the idea of God beyond the creation and beyond humanity.

These are two complementary visions and we have to bring them together in our lives, so that each enriches the other. Theology today is concerned with discerning the relationship between these different visions. Until recently it was the custom to dismiss all other religions as false. Now we are faced with these religions which claim the same kind of absoluteness which Christianity does. I once had a meeting with a learned Hindu pandit, a learned Muslim, principal of a college, and a Zoroastrian. It was instructive to see the way each one said that all religions were good and he appreciated them, but his religion was the supreme one. That is the normal attitude, and that is the sort of thing we have to overcome. We have to try to see our own religion in its relation to other religions; and we will find, and do find, something unique in each religion.

Each one has to recognize the uniqueness of his own religion, and then to relate it to the other religions with their claims to give salvation, to set man free from this world, to bring him everlasting life, or liberation. This is the challenge which is offered us.

I hope that in these six talks we can go through at least the main texts and give an outline of the Hindu doctrine in the Upanishads and in the Bhagavad-Gita, and then try to see what is distinctive in the Christian revelation, and how we relate this to God's revelation among other people. I feel that this is something which the Church today must undertake. It cannot any longer ignore the power, the influence and the depth of these other traditions. Whether we take the Semitic religions — Judaism, Islam and Christianity — or the Oriental religions — Hinduism, Buddhism, Taoism, Confucianism — we see two hemispheres, two totally different approaches to God, to Reality, to the ultimate Truth. And my conviction is that they are complementary.

We have reached a stage in human history where these two hemispheres, these two complementary approaches, have to meet and to share. I believe that the future of the Church is in this meeting with the Oriental tradition. When the Church came out of Judea and Palestine it was a little Jewish sect, speaking Aramaic, worshipping according to Jewish custom, and entirely immersed in its Jewish world. It went out into the Greco-Roman empire, and discovered the profound philosophy of the Greeks, and the Roman empire with its laws and organization. Within five centuries it had come to terms with those traditions. Christian theology was a result of this meeting of the Jewish tradition with Greek philosophy. Christians still use the words of Greek philosophy when speaking of the Trinity, in terms of persons and nature, and of substance and accident in the Eucharist. It is the language of the fathers of the Church, who were students of Greek philosophy. In the same way, when the Church entered the Roman empire, she accepted the divisions of the Roman empire — we still talk about dioceses. A diocese was a province of the Roman empire. It is fascinating the way this whole Greco-Roman structure was built into the Church, so that it has inherited Semitic revelation with a Greco-Roman structure.

Today, I believe, the Church is being called to hold fast to the truth which has been received through the Bible, and through the Greco-Roman tradition, but also to open up to different cultural traditions. African tradition, for instance, has an immense amount to give to the Church. But above all Christians must pay attention to the religions of Asia. These religions have existed for more than three thousand years. They are older than Christianity; they still stand with absolute firmness and show signs of growth rather than of disintegration.

There is great hope that the Christian faith can be enriched and enlarged by contact with these religions. Each religion has its limitations and defects, and each has to answer this challenge. Without Christianity I do not think the Oriental religions can answer the needs of the modern world. But without the enrichment of the mystical tradition of Asia I doubt whether the Western Churches can really discover the fullness of Christ. We have to meet and to share. That is the goal which I believe we should pursue.

The Cosmic Covenant

N ow we come to reflect on the Cosmic Covenant. In the previous talk I spoke about the Vedic Revelation in order to try to place it in the perspective of Biblical Revelation. This is, as I was saying, something new to many people — how to relate to revelation outside the Church. Surely we have a wonderful indication of the nature of this revelation when we reflect on the Cosmic Covenant.

In the Bible the priestly writer, as he is called, divided biblical history, the history of God's revelation, into a series of covenants. First of all there was the covenant with Adam. This covenant with Adam is the covenant with Man. The Bible is concerned with God's relation with Man from the beginning. However far we have to extend the creation of man, maybe to millions of years, it is still covered by this Cosmic Covenant where God has related Himself to mankind. The word *adam* in Hebrew simply means 'man.' God has been calling man from the beginning of time, and that is the Cosmic Covenant.

This Cosmic Covenant originated in Paradise. Paradise is that state where man is in harmony both with nature and with God. The Christian Church has always looked back to an original state of harmony. Man was called to be in harmony with nature, with himself and with God. That surely is what we today, perhaps more than ever, realize we have lost. The terrible conflict with nature which we experience today, the whole problem in ecology, is the fruit of the loss of that original harmony. Likewise we experience the lack of man's harmony with man in wars and violence, crime, and all human conflict. Finally, we have the severed communion between man and God, which is the source of the whole of this conflict. That is the traditional Christian background: the original harmony of man with nature, of man with himself and of man and nature with God. Original Sin is the loss of this primordial harmony, and the Bible looks forward to a new creation when once more this harmony will be restored. Christ is the one who restores the whole creation. "If anyone is in Christ," as St Paul says, "there is a new creation."

We begin with the Covenant with Adam and then we go on to the very significant covenant with Noah. Before God revealed Himself in a special revelation to the Jews, to Moses, to David, and to the prophets, He revealed Himself to Noah, and in the Hebrew understanding Noah was the father of mankind. Mankind had been destroyed in the flood; a new mankind, foretelling the new creation, came into being and Noah was the father of this new mankind. His three sons represented all the nations of the world known to Israel: Shem the Semitic people; Ham the Hamitic (perhaps the Egyptians and Canaanites); and Japheth the islanders, the Greeks and others. Their knowledge was limited, but the point of the story is that Noah is the father of mankind and God made a covenant through Noah with all mankind. This covenant with Noah is the new expression of the Cosmic Covenant.

I feel it is very important for us today to realize that no one is outside this covenant with God. That is why Christians now speak of the various religions of the world as being within the plan of God rather than outside His plan. All are included within this Cosmic Covenant. The Bible itself has a record of the covenant God made with man before He made a special covenant with Israel, and this includes all the ancient patriarchs, beginning with Abel, Seth and Enoch. Enoch, it is said, was a righteous man and he walked with God. The old translation says: "He was not, for God took him," i.e. God took him up to heaven. So here is a holy man, a pagan, who is so close to God that it is believed he was taken up to heaven and the Jews expected that he would return, as is shown in the Apocalypse of Enoch, written a little before the time of Christ.

And then we come to Noah, the father of mankind, with the explicit statement: "I make a covenant with thee and with all flesh." Later, in the fourteenth chapter of Genesis, appears that most interesting figure, Melchizedek. Melchizedek is said to have been a priest and a king of Salem, later Jerusalem, but a pagan priest. He meets Abraham and makes a covenant with him, saying: "I lift up my hand to the most high God, the creator of heaven and earth." *El Elyon* is the Hebrew for the 'most high God.' That is the name by which the God of Israel was known to the Gentiles. In the New Testament this still survives with the Syro-Phoenician woman when she cries out to Jesus: "Jesus, son of the most high God!" So the Jews recognized a "most high God" among the Gentiles, and the Gentiles recognized the God of Israel as this "most high God." Melchizedek says: "I lift up my hand to the most high God, creator of heaven and earth," and Abraham replies: "I lift up my hand to the most high God." So he recognizes the God of Melchizedek. This is very important: in the beginning of the biblical tradition there was this recognition that God had revealed Himself to the Gentiles, to what were later called "pagans."

This led Newman to write a remarkable dissertation on the "dispensation of paganism." There is a dispensation of paganism included in the plan of God. This is extremely significant for us today, as we come to know more of the different peoples of the world. In America there is an awakening to the reality of the American Indians. They have a marvelous tradition of wisdom, inherited from past ages, which was simply rejected before; now we are rediscovering that God has revealed Himself to the American Indians. We find the same with the Australian aborigines. I remember meeting an Australian sculptor who devoted his life to the study of the aborigines. He said that he was amazed at the depth of wisdom he had found in their myths, their traditions, their whole way of life.

All over the world we are rediscovering this pagan religion, this dispensation of paganism. Melchizedek is a priest of this cosmic religion. Now, to crown it all, in the Psalms the Messiah is said to be "a priest forever of the order of Melchizedek" — not of the order of Aaron, of the Jewish priesthood, but of Melchizedek, this 'pagan' priesthood. This is surely of immense significance: that Christ comes to fulfill not only God's revelation to Israel, Moses, David and the prophets, but also the whole of this cosmic covenant, this cosmic revelation.

That is why, when I enter a Hindu temple, I feel that I am entering a holy place, because I regard Hinduism as a cosmic religion. The sacrifices offered there are equivalent to the sacrifice of Melchizedek. We must recognize that God is present among such people, in a way different, no doubt, from the way He is present in a church, but in a way that is as real as his presence to Melchizedek.

Finally, one may mention the Book of Job, which is a crucial book in the Old Testament, written at the time of the captivity about a holy pagan. Three holy pagans are mentioned in Ezekiel — Noah, Daniel and Job. The Book of Job was written to show that this holy man, who was of the land of Hus, not of the land of Israel, was justified in the sight of God.

In the Old Testament, therefore, there is a definite concept of a cosmic covenant made with all men. In his little book, *The Holy Pagans of the Old Testament*, Jean Danielou explains the content of this cosmic revelation. He says that it is God's revelation in nature or creation, and in the soul or the conscience. It has been the constant teaching of the Church, as declared at the First Vatican Council, that God is made known through the creation of the world. As St Paul put it in his letter to the Romans: "His invisible nature is made known by the visible things He has made." This has always been the mode of revelation to primeval man from the beginning. The world which surrounds him is for him a sign of the creator. That is God's primary revelation.

Secondly, God reveals Himself in the heart of man. Again, in the second chapter of the letter to the Romans, where St Paul was dealing with the question of the Gentiles, he said: "The Gentiles who have not the law of Moses have a law written in their hearts: their conscience accusing or perhaps excusing them until the day when God will judge the world by Jesus Christ." This revelation of God in the heart and conscience is the other sign of God to mankind. This again is extremely important today, because we live in a world where the majority of the people are non-Christians. And when we take the Marxist countries into account we find vast numbers of people who no longer believe in God, yet seek to follow their conscience. There again the Second Vatican Council emphasized: "Even those who do not acknowledge God and yet seek to follow their conscience, they also can be saved." So there we have the Cosmic Covenant — God's revelation in the whole creation and God's revelation in the heart of man. No man, no human being is excluded from this covenant.

For those who are Christians, God's revelation comes in the end through Jesus Christ. Therefore we have to say that no one is outside the Christian revelation, in the sense that

Christ died for all men without exception, and the grace of Christ, through the cross, is offered in some way to every human being from the beginning to the end of time. Therefore no one is outside this dispensation, this covenant of grace.

I would like to illustrate this Cosmic Covenant by an example from the book *Patterns of Comparative Religion*, by Mircea Eliade. He is one of the best-known masters of comparative religion. He lectured in Chicago and this book was one of his earlier works but certainly one of the most comprehensive. I have never forgotten a passage there where he shows how primitive man could come to an almost total understanding of God simply by looking at the sky. Early man had not acquired the habit of abstract thought. As I mentioned in the previous talk the thought of primitive man had an intuitive character. He saw the physical, the psychological, and the spiritual worlds in their integrated wholeness. He had not learned to separate man from nature and nature from God.

Consequently, when he looked up at the sky, the sky was a revelation to him. It was not merely the physical phenomenon which we see; to him the sky had a psychological meaning and a spiritual meaning. It revealed the creator present in his creation.

First of all the sky is something vast. It is infinitely above us — we are very small here on earth, while surrounded by this great vastness. God has this vastness, this immensity, and it was revealed to early man through the sky.

Secondly, the sky has no apparent limit. If we look around, everywhere things have their limit: the earth, the trees, animals and people, the clouds in the sky, the sun, the moon, the stars — they all have their limits. But the sky is all-embracing. The sky is without limit. It gives an idea of infinity.

Then again, everything in this world is changing. Things

come into being and they die. The sun rises and sets, the moon waxes and wanes, the seasons change, the clouds come and go, night is succeeded by day. This is a world of continuous change, but behind this world of change there is the unchanging sky. So the sky gives a sense of immensity, of infinity, of eternity.

Then there is an order in the sky. The sun and the moon do not rise without order. In Sanskrit we have the word *rita*, which is the same as the English 'rite.' It means order, harmony, very much the same as the Chinese *Tao*, the order of heaven. So *rita* is the cosmic order, and the two words which determine the moral character of the Vedas more than anything else are *rita* and *satya*. *Rita* is the order of nature, the cosmic order; and *satya* is the truth. It is these two words which in the Vedas express the sense of the Supreme Order of Reality.

So there is a cosmic order. And of course, the more the stars were studied, the more it became clear that there is order in the heavens. Therefore the sky, so vast, so infinite, so eternal and unchanging, is the source of all order. It brings day and night, spring and summer, autumn and winter, the whole order of creation. Therefore the sky is a sovereign being, the Lord of Order.

Again, all good things come down from the sky. First of all the light and heat of the sun, which makes everything germinate on earth. Then the rain comes down from the sky and fertilizes the earth. So the sky, this supreme reality or whatever word we want to give it in modern language, is a source of providence. It provides for man. St Paul appealed to this principle in his sermon to the pagan people at Lystra when he said, "God did not leave Himself without witness — he sent the rain from heaven."

So the sky is provident. And finally the sky is to be feared, because of the thunder and lightning. One wakes up suddenly hearing this terrible roaring in the sky, and one is filled with fear that the lightning may strike. And so this God is to be feared — not with a servile fear, but with that awe with which man approaches God, stands before God.

So the image of the sky can give rise to the image of a god who is immense, infinite, eternal, the source of order, of providence and of fear. This fear implied also a sense of judgement. Primitive man thought that the striking of the lightning was the judgement of God, since God was acting in every event. Of course, this could lead to a superstitious fear, when fear is not related to the sense of order and providence, but behind it lies the cosmic revelation, God revealing Himself in creation. This is an example of how God reveals Himself to all men.

There is an extremely interesting philological argument to support this. In the Vedas there is a very ancient god who soon disappeared — most Indians have never heard of him — called *Dyaus Pita. Dyaus* means 'sky.' The English 'sky' comes from the same root, *dy* and 'sky' are really the same word. *Pita* means father. So *dyaus pita* was the Sky Father. In Greece this became *Zeus Pater; dios pater* and in Latin Jupiter. And when Jesus wanted to teach his disciples to pray, what were the words He used? "Our Father in the sky."

We must never forget, as I was saying before, that for ancient man the sky was never a material thing. It was the abode of the gods. In Jesus' time also the heavens were not just a material thing. It is only since the 16th and 17th century that man has begun to think that things like the earth and the sky are merely material. Certainly they are material, but behind that material reality there are conscious beings whom the ancients called the gods or angels. Saint Thomas and the whole medieval world believed that God ruled the world through the angels, that is, the "cosmic powers." The angels were present in the whole creation, particularly in the stars, the sun and the moon and all the "host of heaven." The sky was not simply a material thing, it was the abode of the gods, the manifestation of the Supreme Spirit, the Supreme Father, who ruled over all. This is how man in prehistoric ages gradually discovered the mystery of the Cosmic Lord and Father of Creation.

We ourselves have not gone beyond this. We have fallen below it. For modern man to speak of God in the sky is absurd. As Khruschev said: "Our pilots have gone far into the sky and they have not found God anywhere there." It is the absurdity of the twentieth century mind to imagine that there is nothing but the material world out there — no god, no angels, no supreme reality. But for a Christian as for others who have a religious mind there is the "Father in heaven" to whom we all pray.

I would like to illustrate this from Hinduism, which to my mind is the supreme example of a cosmic religion. There we have the worship of God revealed through the powers of nature. The *devas*, literally 'the shining ones,' are these cosmic powers manifesting themselves in the whole creation. In Hinduism the supreme Reality is known as Brahman, and this Brahman, the One Being, manifests himself in the devas, the gods, the powers which rule the creation. There is a whole hierarchy, from the Supreme Being, the Cosmic Lord, who transcends all, through all the devas, the powers of nature, to man and his intelligence and his senses, and finally to the world which is below him. So the Hindus have this sense of a hierarchy of being, as the West had in the Middle Ages. But while we have lost it, it is still present in Hinduism.

This can be seen in Hindu temples. The Hindu temple is meant to be a shrine of God. It is not at all like a Christian church. The Christian church is a place for the assembly of the people. Christianity is a community religion and I think this is one of its great values. It has a corporate unity, which is manifested in the Church as the body of Christ.

There is little of this present in Hinduism. Hinduism is an individualistic religion — each one goes to God in his own way. When he visits a temple he goes as an individual, or he may go with his family, but even so every member of the family is worshipping by himself.

On entering a temple one finds a large tank of water for bathing. This represents the purgative way. One cleanses oneself from sin; that is the first thing to do on entering the temple.

Next there is a very interesting ceremony: At the entrance of the temple there is a figure of the god Ganesh, the elephant god. He is a very quaint figure, with an elephant's head and a fat belly, much loved by all Hindus. His fundamental characteristic is his power of removing obstacles. He is also called *Vināyaka*, 'the one who removes obstacles.' Whenever they want to undertake a journey or a marriage or anything of importance they pray to Ganesh to remove the obstacles. So on entering the temple they break a coconut before the shrine of Ganesh. Now, breaking a coconut is a beautiful action. A coconut has a hard, rough exterior and inside there is a white substance and sweet milk. The outer nutshell is the external self, the ego. They break their ego. Inside is the pure white substance, the sweet milk symbolizing the divine life within. So they try to remove all the obstacles from the mind and make it open to God. That is the first stage.

Then they go around to all the courts of the temple. There are many shrines of different gods all around which represent the cosmic powers and they relate themselves to all of these, to the whole cosmic order, trying to be in harmony with the universe. So while going around, they pay their devotions at the different shrines. This represents the illuminative way, the path of God revealing Himself in the cosmos.

Finally one comes to what is called the *garbha griha*, the

'house of the womb,' the source of life, or the *mulasthanam*, the inner sanctuary which is always dark. The meaning of this is that God, the ultimate mystery, dwells in the darkness, beyond the light of this world. In the little temple in our ashram we follow the same pattern: the inner sanctuary is always kept in darkness with only an oil lamp burning before the tabernacle.

So going to the temple means leaving the outer world behind, going through a purification, uniting with all the powers of the cosmos and finally entering into the inner shrine of the Self where God dwells in the darkness. At that point one experiences union with God. It is a beautiful symbolism, a beautiful example of cosmic religion and cosmic worship.

The Hindu puja is another example. I mentioned earlier that the typical rite of the Vedas was the fire sacrifice. I have seen several fire sacrifices, but they are rare and are performed only on great occasions. When the new temple was dedicated in our local village seven altars were built and Brahmin priests were invited from various parts of the country to perform this sacred ritual which took many days. That was the old Vedic fire sacrifice. Today it is a rarity — the ordinary worship in the temple is called *puja*. A typical puja consists in offering the elements to God as a sign of the offering of the creation — earth, water, air and fire. It can be performed in a big temple with many pujaris and big crowds, or in a tiny village shrine among poor people, but it is always basically the same rite.

First of all they will put out some food on a plantain leaf, the fruits of the earth, rice with maybe a lemon, or some sugar cane. Then they will purify it with water. They make an offering of water, sprinkling it around the food which is to be offered to God, thus purifying it. Then they take incense, place it in a bowl and wave it over the offering; this is called *arati* and signifies the offering of the air. Then camphor is burnt, which signifies the offering of fire. Camphor burns with a pure flame; it burns itself out without leaving any residue. This is taken as a symbol of the soul burning itself out in the service of God. This light is also waved around the offering. In this way the four elements are offered to God in the form of a cosmic sacrifice.

In the mass of the Indian rite which we celebrate in our ashram we try to adapt ourselves to this form of sacrifice. At the offertory we first sprinkle water around the gifts and the altar. Then we sprinkle water on the people and then the priest takes a sip of water to purify himself within. Thus we begin with the offering of water. Then we take the fruits of the earth, bread and wine. There is a beautiful prayer in the new liturgy: "Blessed are you, Lord God of all creation! Through your goodness we have this bread to offer which earth has given and human hands have made." Thus we offer the fruits of the earth and the work of human hands to the Divine. Then we take eight flowers and place them around the gifts in the eight directions of space to signify that the sacrifice we offer is at the centre of the universe. Every sacrifice in the ancient world was conceived as being offered at the centre of the universe. They always related themselves to the whole cosmos. Then we take incense and wave it over the gifts and in the same way we wave the fire, the flame of burning camphor over them.

This fourfold offering of the elements is to signify that the mass is a cosmic sacrifice. Christ has assumed the whole creation. He is offering it in and through himself to his Father. He has not only taken us up into himself; he has taken up the whole of creation.

This is why the cosmic covenant has such importance for us. It enlarges our vision. We have become too human, too limited in our vision of life; we forget this great cosmic order through which God reveals himself all the time and which should be manifested in the Church. In this cosmic sacrifice the whole creation is offered in and through Christ to the Father.

I have mentioned that everything in India has a sacred character. This is what people who come from the West find so moving. It meets one on every side — they are living in a sacred world. Here in the West we live in a profane world. For the last three centuries we have tried to remove everything from the sphere of the sacred, the sphere of God. This has its value — the sphere of the sacred can also be the sphere of superstition, an obstacle to progress. Therefore science tries to eliminate the sacred: the moon is not something sacred at all, it is simply a chemical formation, and we want to learn all we can about it. It is the same with the earth, and with everything else. This approach has its own value, but we have eliminated two dimensions of reality, the psychological and the spiritual. We only conceive reality from that one particular point. Having removed the others, we begin to think that this world is one-dimensional, that it is only material — we forget the sacred character of the whole creation.

This sacred character is always present in Hinduism. Every meal is sacred. In a devout household they put their food on a plantain leaf. They don't need any utensils, they use the hands God gave them. On the leaf they put rice and vegetables and this food is considered to be something sacred. This is also one of the reasons for many superstitions. The kitchen is a sacred place in the Hindu household and no outsider is allowed to enter, for if an impure person went into the kitchen all the food would be polluted.

I heard a story once about a great marriage which was to take place. All the women in the household were busy preparing the food. Although a woman may not have an important place in public life in India, in the home she is the queen. She is the mistress of the household, and no man is allowed to interfere in her domain. There was a European in that village who had been invited to the wedding. Of course he did not know all their customs, so by accident he put a foot in the kitchen, with the result that all the food had to be thrown away. They couldn't use it anymore, everything had been polluted by that stranger's foot in the kitchen.

Behind this extreme sensitivity is a sense of the sacredness of food. Normally a Hindu housewife, in preparing the food, will put aside a certain portion of rice for a stranger who may come, and a stranger represents God. It is God who comes in the stranger, and some food is always put aside for him.

So food is sacred. You put it on a plantain leaf and the first thing you do is take some water in your hands and sprinkle it around the plantain leaf. You make a sacred space and purify it, to keep away all evil forces which are around. Like our own forefathers the Hindus are convinced that both good and evil forces surround us all the time and that we must be aware of the evil forces as well as of the good. So you purify your food, and then offer it in sacrifice.

When you take the food into your mouth, it goes down into the stomach and it is consumed in the "fire of the stomach." This fire is a sacred fire. There is a verse in the Bhagavad-Gita which we chant after the meals in our ashram:

Aham vaisvanaro bhutva
praninam deham asritah
pranapana samayuktah
pachamy annam chaturvidham.

"I become the fire of life in the bodies of living creatures and mingling with the upward and downward breath, I consume the four kinds of food." It is the Lord who receives your offering and converts it into a spiritual reality. Your food is a sacrament.

As your bath and your food, so also your work is sacred. When we want to put up a new building in the ashram, we send for the workers. They come and make all the necessary preparations, and then they choose a propitious day and hour. At the appropriate time they perform certain rites. I am called to sprinkle holy water and say a prayer. They would never begin to put up a building without some kind of consecration.

We once helped to start a weavers' cooperative in the village — the hand-loom weavers there do beautiful work — and I would go to the meetings from time to time. Every meeting began with prayer and offerings, and when the account books were produced, every book had a little sandalwood mark to make it sacred: it was like a sacrament. Even the account books must be sacred. So here we are, in a world of sacramentality, of sacramental work. That is the world of the cosmic religion.

Now we come to the second part of the cosmic revelation, the cosmic revelation in the heart of man. It goes deeper still. Here the figure of Shiva Nataraja, the Dancing Shiva, is so profoundly interesting. He is one of the great figures of Indian mythology. He is represented with four arms dancing in a circle of fire, dancing at the heart of creation. It is a cosmic dance: it represents the power which permeates the whole universe. The idea is that God is dancing in the heart of creation and in every human heart. We must find the Lord who is dancing in our hearts; then we will see the Lord dancing in all of creation. There are many symbols contained in the figure of Shiva. The first is the drum which he holds in his upper right hand. That is the sign of creation, of the vibration of sound from which creation comes. The word *om* is held to be the original sound. It is a little like the Greek alpha and omega, the beginning and the end which embraces all words, all meaning, all sound, all creation itself.

So in the upper right hand he holds the drum, the symbol of creation, the vibration of sound from which the world comes; and in his upper left hand he holds fire, the symbol of destruction. The Hindu is very realistic: he sees the whole world as continually being created and destroyed. Everything is coming into being and is dying. Birth and death and re-birth goes on all the time. This is the rhythm of creation, the order of creation which is sustained by God. As we accept this coming into being we also accept the passing out of being — the creation and the destruction.

With his lower right hand Shiva makes a beautiful gesture called the *abhaya mudra*, the symbol of the removal of fear. This idea of fearlessness is one of the great principles in the *sannyasa* tradition, which is something like the monastic tradition in the West. When a disciple is finally given status as a sannyasi, he is told to go hence, let him fear nothing and let no one be afraid of him, neither animals nor men. We find the same thing among the fathers of the desert as in the story of St Jerome and his lion. Many sannyasis live in caves, and snakes come and coil around their legs. But they sit unmoving, and the snakes go away because they have no fear.

Shiva's lower left hand points towards his foot which is the source of grace. It sounds strange, but in India you always go for refuge to the foot of the Lord. In the same way, when you approach a sannyasi or any revered person you bow down and touch his feet. The feet are the source of grace. And so the foot of the Lord is the way he expresses grace. He says, "Come to me for the grace of your salvation."

The whole figure can be seen as a beautiful symbol of the Risen Christ. Christ is at the heart of the universe. St Paul says, "In and through and for Him all things consist. All things hold together in Him." He sustains the whole universe. This holding of the universe is a kind of dance, the dance of the universe, and He is dancing in every human heart. You have to recognize the Lord dancing in your heart and then you dance with Him. There's a popular song: "The Lord of the Dance" which brings out this idea. This is another example of cosmic religion.

The Lord reveals Himself in the whole creation and He reveals Himself in the human heart. We will be going on to the Upanishads which are largely concerned with this revelation in the heart, so I will not go into that now. But one last word: God's manifestation in the world of creation is commonly attributed to Brahma, Vishnu and Shiva. They are three forms of God. Brahma is the Creator, Vishnu the preserver and Shiva the destroyer.

Brahma is the creative god; and here we must distinguish between *Brahma*, the masculine, the figure of the creator, and *Brahman* which is neuter and signifies the Supreme Reality, the One beyond everything. So Brahma is the figure of the creator.

Vishnu is the figure of the preserver. He is the one who pervades the whole creation. God pervades every grain of matter, every living thing, every human being. Everything is pervaded by God. People sometimes speak of this as pantheism. It is not pantheism. It can be called panentheism. God is *in* everything. I like to recall how St Thomas Aquinas asked, "In what way is God in the creation?" and he answered, "First of all God is in the whole creation by His power, because He sustains everything by His power." That is an obvious Christian doctrine. The whole creation is held in being by the power of God. In Sanskrit it is known as *shakti*, the 'Power of God.' But then he goes on to say that God does not exercise His power at a distance, because in God there is no distance. Therefore, He is in everything by His Presence. God is present in everything. And furthermore He is not present as it were as a part of Himself, because there are no parts of God. He is present in His essence.

So the divine essence, the Holy Trinity, is totally present in every particle of matter, every atom, and every electron; however you would like to divide the universe, the whole creation is totally pervaded by God. The cosmic religion has this awareness of God pervading the whole creation which we, as a whole, have lost. The Hindu is still aware of the Divine Immanence in the universe.

Shiva is the destroyer. That sounds forbidding, but obviously there are forces of destruction in nature which we have to accept. These forces are represented by Shiva and Kali. Kali is the consort of Shiva; she is the mother goddess who is the great destroyer. One finds pictures of her, hung with skulls and snakes, holding out her tongue, devouring the whole creation. This destructive element is in all nature. But the Hindu sees that behind all this destruction is also re-creation. So Mother Kali is also the mother of creation and therefore she is worshipped also as the goddess of infinite love. She is the source of death and destruction, but she is also the source of grace. There is always both a positive and a negative aspect which we have to recognize. In Shiva the symbolism also develops in this way. He is the destroyer of the world but he is also the one who destroys sin and converts by his grace. This is obviously very close to the Christian conception of divine grace. This is the way the cosmic revelation has developed in India.

Finally, we could say that this Brahma-Vishnu-Shiva is a remote analogy of the Trinity, a very remote one, no doubt. Its function is not that of the proper Trinity, since it signifies an external not an internal relationship, and we should not confuse it in any way, but it is an indication of a triple character in God. Deeper than that there is the conception of God as Brahman.

There is the infinite transcendent reality called *Nirguna Brahman*, without qualities, without attributes, beyond everything which can be conceived. That is Nirguna Brahman.

Then there is *Saguna Brahman*, God with attributes. He is conceived as Creator, as Lord, as Saviour — all these are attributes of God. That is the other aspect of God, as the Lord related to the universe.

Thirdly, God dwells in each person as his own inner spirit, as his Atman. That is the Self within. So, it can be said, in a sense, that Nirguna Brahman is the Father, the Source, the Origin from which everything comes, the Beyond. The Father manifests Himself in the Son, in the Word, who is Saguna Brahman, the self-manifestation of God, the Lord, the Saviour, who manifests himself in all creation. And finally God is present in every human being, in his own innermost spirit, the Spirit of God in man, and this Spirit is the Self-communication of God. That is the Atman. Sometimes, to make it clear that the word is used of the ultimate reality, it is called the *Parabrahman*, the Supreme Brahman, or *Paramatman*, the Supreme Spirit.

The relation of this cosmic revelation to Christ and Christian revelation may be compared to that of the Old Testament in relation to the New. One does not find the doctrine of the Trinity either, nor properly speaking the doctrine of the incarnation, but nevertheless the elements are there. There is a presence of the Father, the Son and the Holy Spirit, though their relationship is not recognized. In all these centuries God has been guiding those people who meditate on Him, who realize His presence in the whole of creation and in their hearts, and seek to express it in myth and symbol. All these myths and images are symbols of man's searching for God, searching to understand the mystery of man and the universe. That is what we want to keep in mind all the time — this constant search for God, for an experience of His presence in the heart, which we seek to relate to God's self manifestation in Christ, in the Holy Spirit and in the Church. We have in the concept of the cosmic revelation the basis for an understanding of the relation of Oriental religion to the mystery of Christ. Christ adds a new dimension to both the Hebrew revelation, God's revelation in the history of Israel, and God's revelation in the cosmos and humanity.

The Cosmic Mystery
(Upanishads)

We are going to reflect on the Cosmic Mystery in the Upanishads. When we approach the Upanishads for an understanding of the Cosmic Mystery, we are coming to the very heart of the Hindu experience of God. This is what we want to try to understand, not with our minds, but with our hearts: to enter into the heart and continually remind ourselves that the Upanishads are intended to lead us to the heart. The Greek fathers of the Church used to say, "Lead the thoughts from the head into the heart and keep them there." This is to open the heart to the Cosmic Mystery.

In theory there are a hundred and eight Upanishads. It is a sacred number and they accumulated over the centuries, but actually there are only twelve classical Upanishads. They date from the sixth century, B.C., and these are the only ones which will concern us seriously. Of these, there are two early ones, rather long and in prose, called the *Brihadaranyaka* and the *Chandogya*. They are difficult, but also among the richest and the most original of the Upanishads. Then there is a whole series of short Upanishads, beginning with the *Isa*, followed by the *Kena, Katha, Mandukya, Mundaka, Prasna*, and *Svetasvatara*. Those who are interested in studying the Upanishads can easily read these and find in them all that they need to know. One of the most important of these is the Svetasvatara Upanishad that comes toward the end of the

47

third century. It is called a theistic Upanishad, because it is centred on the concept of a personal God.

In our study of the Upanishads I want to concentrate on three words which signify the Godhead, the One Being. This One Being, this Cosmic Mystery, is beyond all names. However, the three words which signify it are Brahman, Atman, and Purusha. Perhaps we cannot do better than to begin with a text from the Brihadaranyaka, the Great Forest Upanishad. As I said, these Upanishads are derived from the meditations of the seers in the forest, and in the first book of the Brihadaranyaka there are two revealing sentences. The first one is, "Verily, in the beginning this was Brahman, one only." Brahman is the source of the whole creation. This world was Brahman in the sense that it is grounded in Brahman, and he is one only. They often say *Ekam eva advitya*, 'one only without a second.'

And then another sentence reads, "In the beginning, this was the Atman, the Spirit, alone in the form of a Purusha, a Person." In these three words: *Brahman, Atman,* the 'Self' or 'Spirit,' and *Purusha,* 'Person,' we can see how the Hindu came to understand the Mystery of the Cosmos. First of all, looking round on the world he discovered Brahman as the ground of all being; then he discovered the Atman, the Self, as the ground of all consciousness; and then he rose to the conception of the Purusha and saw how Brahman, Atman, and Purusha, the Personal God, are all one. In this talk we will concentrate on Brahman and Atman.

The word *Brahman* comes from the root *Brh*, which is believed to mean 'to grow or to swell.' We must remember that there is never merely a physical meaning; there is always a psychological and a spiritual meaning to a word. This swelling seems to be the rising up of the awareness of God. The word Brahman came to mean a prayer, something which rises up in the heart, swells within, breaks out and opens up to the divine, to a mystery beyond. Man is in search of this hidden mystery, and it is a mystery which cannot be named. This must always be remembered: Brahman cannot properly be named. It is without name or form. We use words to point to the mystery, but we can never express it. That is why we have to be careful in reading the Upanishads not to take them simply in a literal sense. They point us towards an inexpressible mystery, and the word which expresses that mystery, more than anything else, is this word *Brahman*. Originally it meant 'prayer,' or 'mantra,' the 'word' that rose up in the sacrifice. You were offering your sacrifice, and then your heart swells, as it were, and you want to open yourself to God, to offer to God the word which came forth, the mantra. In the early literature of the Vedas that is the common meaning of Brahman. It is a prayer, or a mantra, a sacred word.

In the Vedas, as I said, the sacrifice was the centre of the whole religion. We must never forget this: sacrifice was the centre of all ancient religion. In the Vedas it is very clear that everything comes down from above, from heaven. We receive everything from above and everything must be returned. A sacrifice is the return to God, and sin is the opposite, the appropriation of something to one's self. We say, "This is mine. I can do what I like," but in fact this is God's gift, and I am responsible and have to return it to Him. It applies to everything, to every person, and to myself. I am not my own possession; I am a gift — my being is a gift from God. I have got to return that gift. Sacrifice is this return. Its purpose is to make a thing sacred, to return it to God.

As the sacrifice was considered to be the source of life for the whole creation, the whole creation was held to depend on sacrifice: it came forth from God and returned to God. That is the *rita*, the 'order,' that is the rhythm of the world — the coming forth from God and the returning to God.

When you live in that rhythm you are said to turn the wheel

of the law, the *dharma chakra*. When you live as you should, you are turning the wheel of the law. When you sin, you are going against that rhythm, that law of the universe. The sacrifice is the support of the whole world, and therefore as the Brahman, the mantra, the word of sacrifice was the centre of the sacrifice, so it came to be the centre, the source, the principle of the whole creation.

Brahman is that power which sustains the sacrifice and sustains the whole creation. It is ultimately the mystery of creation. There are three aspects of this which are brought out very clearly. The first is that Brahman is the source of everything. Here there are various images, and again we must be careful not simply to take these images literally. There are two in particular; one is: "As a spider comes out with its thread, so this whole universe comes out from Brahman." And another is, "As sparks come out from a fire, so this whole universe comes out from Brahman."

If that is taken literally it is a form of pantheism; the world and God are the same, or the world is a part of God; many have interpreted it like that. Professor Zaehner in the book I mentioned, *The Hindu Scriptures*, refers to the teachings of the Upanishads as a 'pantheistic monism.' He explains that it is pantheistic because it holds that all is God, and it is monist because it says that there is only one reality, one being. I think that this is a complete misconception. I hope to make it clear that Hindu teaching is infinitely deeper. It is neither pantheistic nor monistic. It is only too common to be told by European scholars that Hinduism is pantheistic or monistic. I am not denying that the language is sometimes pantheistic or monistic and that some Hindu schools showed pantheistic and monistic tendencies, but the essential teaching is neither the one nor the other. These are Greek words, and they do not apply to the Hindu understanding of God.

Brahman is the source; the whole universe comes forth

from Brahman. That is the first point. He is the source from which everything comes. The second point is that Brahman pervades the universe.

There is a beautiful text here. The Upanishads always make their point in the form of stories and with illustrations which are very attractive. In the early Vedic period women were on an equal footing with men. These great discoveries were often discussed between the wife and the husband. Afterwards, women were totally excluded; they were not allowed to read the Vedas, but in early times women took their part. In this story from the Bridharanyaka Upanishad the woman is Gargi, a wife of Yajnavalkya, who was one of the great seers. Gargi asked:

"Everything here is woven, like warp and woof, in water. What then is that in which the water is woven, like warp and woof?" She is trying to find what the source of everything is. One of the earliest Greek philosophers, Thales, said that everything came from water. It was a common view. Water is liquid and it becomes solid in ice and it can become steam when it is boiled. So Gargi starts with water, and asks, "In what is the water woven?" and he replies, "In the air." Then she says, "In what is the air woven?" and he says "In the sky." Then she asks, "In what is the sky woven?" and he replies, "In the Spiritual powers."

Beyond the material is the spiritual world, called the world of the angels, or the world of the gods. He says the whole of this material world is woven on the woof of the heavenly world. And then she asks, "In what is the world of heaven woven?" He says, "It is woven in the Creator." Then she asks, "In what are the worlds of Prajapati, the Creator woven?" and he says, "They are woven in the world of Brahman." And she asks, "In what are the worlds of Brahman woven, like warp and woof?" And he says, "Oh, Gargi, do not ask too much, lest thy head should fall off!"

The Cosmic Revelation

You see, one must come to the end of questioning. We also go on questioning, in the way of modern science; we reduce everything to atoms, then we come to electrons and protons — we are always trying to find what is behind it all. What is it all woven in? At last one comes to something which cannot be named, cannot be seen — the hidden mystery. That is Brahman, on which everything is woven. The world of the gods, the world of the sky and of the earth are all woven on Brahman. He is the One pervading all.

Here is another example. Again it is a woman speaking. Yajnavalkya had two wives. One was Gargi, as we have seen, and the other was called Maitri. He wanted to give up his family and become a Sannyasi, to go into the forest. So he says to his wife, Maitri:

"I am going away from this house into the forest. Let me make a settlement between thee and Gargi." Maitri asks, "My lord, if this whole earth full of wealth belonged to me, should I be immortal by it?" And Yajnavalkya says, "No. Like the life of rich people thy life will be, but there is no hope of immortality by wealth." And then she asks, "But what should I do with that by which I do not become immortal? What does My Lord know of immortality? Tell me that." She is convinced that wealth will not satisfy. She is longing for immortality. This recalls the famous verse of the same Upanishad, "from the unreal lead me to the real, from darkness lead me to light, from death lead me to immortality." That is what they were seeking, immortality. Then Yajnavalkya says, "Thou art truly dear to me. Thou speakest dear words. Come, sit down and I will explain it to thee and meditate on what I say."

Then he begins to speak to her about Brahman and Atman. The words are almost interchangeable in the end. He says: "Verily, a husband is not dear that you may love a husband, but that you may love the Atman, the Spirit, the Self, therefore a husband is dear.'' In the same way he says that it is not for the sake of wife or children or riches that each of these is dear, but for the sake of the Spirit, the Atman, that they are dear. In other words, everything in this world, husbands and wives, children and riches, all come from God, from Brahman, from the Spirit, and they are to be loved in and through the Spirit. It does not mean that you reject your husband or wife, but that you love them in the depth of their being, in the Spirit which is in all. You love them in and through the Atman, the Self which is their very soul, their true being. Every person is to be loved for the sake of that Brahman, who is the source, the pervading principle of all, and the object of all desire.

When we try to express what this Brahman is, of course, it cannot be expressed. But there are two methods of approach to it, one is called the affirmative and the other the negative way. These are the methods of affirmative and negative theology.

First of all, Yajnavalkya uses various images. He asks, ''What is the appearance of that *Purusha*, that 'Person?' '' using the word *Purusha* for the supreme reality. *Brahman, Atman* and *Purusha* are three terms for the one reality. Each has a subtle difference, but the words can also be interchangeable, and in this case, the word *Purusha* is used.

Having asked ''What is the appearance of that person, that Purusha?'' he answers, ''He is like a saffron-colored garment.'' Saffron is the color worn by the sannyasi, the holy man, in India. It is a sign of renunciation, of the passing beyond this world.

Then he says, ''He is like white wool.'' In the Apocalypse of St John when the Lord appeared it is said that his head was white like wool, and in the transfiguration his garments were shining white. ''He is like *cochineal* (the purple dye), like a flame of fire, like a white lotus or like sudden lightning.'' He gives a series of images to awaken the disciple to this mystery — not to express it literally but to awaken us to the mystery.

Then comes what is perhaps the most fundamental teaching of the Upanishads, the teaching of Brahman by *neti, neti,* 'not this, not this.' "There is nothing higher than this, than if one says, 'not this, not this.' " This is negative theology. We cannot name Brahman. It is 'not this, not this.' Whatever word we use, whatever image, whatever concept, we have always to go beyond.

Christians have constantly to remind themselves that one cannot stop with any name of God, however holy the name may be. The name points to the Person, and the Person points to the inexpressible mystery. We are all seeking that inexpressible mystery beyond, and that is Brahman, which is *neti, neti,* 'not this, not this.'

So there we have the foundation. I would put it in this way. When we look around at the world about us, we see the earth, the sky, the water, the plants and trees, the animals, and people. But what we have to do is to look behind all these phenomena and discover their hidden source. Most people stop with the phenomena: they appreciate the earth or sky or flowers or the sun or stars, they admire their beauty, but they do not try to find the hidden source of the sky and the flowers, of every single thing. This was brought out in the Chandogya Upanishad.

It comes in a story about a Brahmin who has a son, Svetaketu. His father tells him, "Svetaketu, go to school, for there is no one belonging to our race, my dear, who not having studied the Vedas, is a Brahmin by birth only."

A Brahmin belongs to one of the four *varnas*. These are not precisely castes — the name for which is *jati* — but rather classes which form the basic structure of society. The first of these was the Brahmin, the priest. His function was to study the Vedas, the sacred scriptures, to learn the *dharma*, the law of life, from the scriptures, and then to teach. For thousands of years there has been in India a class of people whose one function in life was to study the scriptures, to perform the rites of religion and to teach the law of God. It is mainly through this institution that religion has been preserved. Then there is the *Kshatriya*, the warrior, the statesman, the ruler of the society; then the *Vaisya*, the merchant and the farmer; and last of all the *Sudra*, the worker. Though this system is obviously open to every abuse, it has yet preserved the basic structure of society through the ages.

These were the four classes, the four orders of society which were all necessary, one to the other. The Brahmin's function was to study the Vedas, and at the age of twelve he would receive the sacred thread in the *Upanayana* ceremony. This custom is still preserved in India today. It is a solemn ceremony. The whole family gathers round, the little boy is seated in state, and the guru comes to invest him with the sacred thread and to whisper the Gayatri mantra, which we mentioned at the beginning of the first talk, into his ear. This he is supposed to repeat regularly every day as the principal form of his prayer. Then he studies Sanskrit for twelve years, and has to learn the Vedas by heart. In the ancient world they learned everything by heart. The early Benedictine monks and nuns had to learn the Psalms by heart. It was the first thing they did as novices, since there were very few books, and it had great value in strengthening the powers of memory. It is instructive to notice the difference in India today between Christians and Hindus. When Christians come to church they need a multitude of books to follow the service, and all the ceremonies require the use of books. But the Hindus have everything by heart. They can sit down and begin to sing and recite and speak without any books for hours on end. In ancient times they first learned everything by heart, and then they studied the meaning. Thus the Brahmin boy goes and studies, and then he returns to his family.

Svetaketu, the boy in our story, returned to his father when he was twenty-four, having studied all the Vedas. He considered himself very well-read, and very learned. His father asks, "Svetaketu, as you are so conceited, considering yourself so well-read and so learned, my dear, have you ever learned of that instruction by which we hear that which cannot be heard, by which we perceive that which cannot be perceived, and by which we know that which cannot be known?" and the son said, "No, Father, I have not learned that."

That is the crucial question. You can read all the Vedas, just as you can read the whole Bible, and you can know all about the Sanskrit, and the Hebrew, and be able to expound the scriptures in all their details, but you may still not discover the word of God in the Bible, or the hidden mystery in the Vedas. Again and again, it is said, what is the good of all the learning of the Vedas if you do not know this Brahmin, this hidden mystery?

So his father begins to instruct him on this mystery. He uses several simple illustrations. The one which I like best is this: He says, "Go fetch me the fruit of that banyan tree." The son fetches the fruit to him, and he says, "Break the fruit; what do you see?" The son says, "I see a lot of seeds, very small." Then the father says, "Break one of the seeds; what do you see there?" The son replies, "I see nothing." Then the father continues, "My Son, from that subtle essence, which you do not perceive, from that very essence comes this great banyan tree." In the heart of the seed is the hidden mystery which you cannot see, and the whole tree comes forth from this hidden power within. There is a hidden mystery, an energy, a power, which is the source of the whole creation. That which you cannot see, that is the source of the whole. "Believe it, My Son, in that subtle essence all that exists has its self, has its real being, that is the Truth, that is the

Self, and thou, Svetaketu, art that."

This brings us to the deepest mystery of the Upanishads. *Tat tvam asi*, 'Thou art That.' This is one of the *mahavakyas*, 'great sayings,' of the Upanishads. These are the mysterious sayings which can so easily be misunderstood. Another is, *aham Brahmasmi*, 'I am Brahman.' Now most Europeans and Christians believe that means, "I am God," and this sounds like blasphemy. They misunderstand the real meaning — because it is essentially a mystical meaning. In the same way, *Tat tvam asi*, 'Thou art That,' does not mean you are God. Again, there is the third mahavakya, *sarvam khalvidam Brahman asti*, 'All this world is Brahman,' and that, they say, is pantheism. Everything is God. That is taking these words literally and interpreting them in a rationalistic sense. But when we study the Upanishads deeply, we realize that they are seeking to express a mystical experience. What they are really saying is, "I, in the deepest centre, the ground of my being, am one with that Brahman, the source of all creation."

There are two ways in which we can approach this mystery. We can look out on the world around us and recognize behind all the phenomena an underlying mystery, the mystery of being sustaining the whole universe, and this mystery we can then call Brahman. Or, alternately, we can look within ourselves and ask, "What is the source of my being?"

Here we have another beautiful story in the Chandogya Upanishad, about three disciples who come to a master and are told by him, "That Self, which is free from sin, free from old age, from death and grief, from hunger and thirst, which desires nothing but what it ought to desire, and imagines nothing but what it ought to imagine, it is that which we should search out; that which we must try to understand. He who reaches that Self and understands it gains all the world of desires." Man has an intuition that there is something within him which is immortal. He is not satisfied with his mortality, and every religion bears witness to this search for immortality. This is the object of search in this Upanishad. They are seeking the immortal Self; they want to be free from sin, free from death, from hunger and thirst. They want to discover themselves. That is just as true today for people in the West as it was true in India in the sixth century B.C.

So they ask the master, "What is this Self?" and he keeps them waiting for thirty-two years. At the end of thirty-two years he says, "For what purpose have you come to dwell here?" This is significant. We think we have to go to college and get a degree, and then we will know everything we need to know. But in the ancient world you took fuel in your hands and approached a Guru. It meant that you came to serve the master, to light his fire, to cook his food, maybe to milk his cow. You served him. And when he saw you were ready, he imparted the knowledge to you. This is a fundamental principle: you cannot receive this knowledge until you are ready for it. "When the disciple is ready," they say, "the guru appears." So he tests them by keeping them waiting, and then he tells them:

"Go and look at a pool of water, and tell me what you see." They go and look in the water, and they see themselves in the water all dressed up nicely, and they think, "That is my Self," and they come back, saying, "Yes, we have seen ourselves." Then they go away, and they begin to reflect on the difficulty this involves — "The body will waste away; the clothes will decay; this is not the Self we are seeking at all." That self belongs to what is called the waking state. Many people really think that this thing which can be seen and touched, this is me; and there is nothing beyond. But on reflection they realize that this is not the true Self. So they come back, and after another thirty-two years, he says to them:

"The self you see in dreams, that is your real Self." The dreaming self is really the inner self, the self of thoughts, feelings, desires, ambitions, fears, all the inner self of man, the personality.

A great many people think their body is themselves, others think their personality is themselves: "This personality is me, this is my Self." And so thinking they are thoroughly satisfied. But then they begin to reflect, this personality of mine — my thoughts, feelings, desires — is going to pass away when my body decays. This is not the Self I am seeking, it also belongs to the changing world.

So they come back again to the master, and after a further thirty-two years he says (and this may appear very strange), "The self you know in deep sleep, that is your real Self." Now the meaning of that is: when you are in deep sleep, your body is not conscious and your mind, your soul, is not conscious. Yet you are there. What is that which is neither your body, nor your mind, your conscious mind? And so they go away again. But then they think, "That may be so; there is a self there that I cannot perceive, but I am not conscious of it and that is not going to help."

So he tells them to wait another five years, and finally, after a hundred and one years, he tells them the truth. He tells them of what is called the fourth state, *turiya*. Beyond the waking state, beyond the dream state, beyond the state of deep sleep, there is the fourth state in which the true Self may be found. That is what we have to seek for, this inner Self, which is to be known not in the darkness of deep sleep but in the pure light of consciousness.

The basic orientation of the Upanishads is found in the search for this inner Self, this Self beyond the body and beyond the mind. In our western world we have come to think that mind and reason are the supreme powers in man. We control this world by using reason. The material world is brought to subjection by the mind of man through science and technology; man is at the head of creation. For the

The Cosmic Revelation

Hindu and for all ancient wisdom this is *maya*, the 'great illusion.' It is *avidya*, 'ignorance,' to think that the mind is
supreme. What we have to discover is what lies beyond the
mind. It is the hidden mystery, from which the mind and the
whole creation comes. That hidden mystery is called *turiya*,
the fourth state. You look out on the world around you and
you find the hidden mystery of Brahman. You look into your
self, your body and your mind, and within the depths of your
being, beyond your mind, you find this hidden mystery of the
Atman, the Spirit. When you say "I am Brahman," *Aham
Brahmasmi*, what you are saying is that in the inner depths of
my being, beyond my ego, beyond my conscious self, I am
one with this inner Spirit which is also the Spirit of the universe. In Christian terms you have discovered yourself in
God. My true Self is my self in God and God in me. I am not
really my Self until I have discovered this hidden centre of my
being.

In the Taittiriya Upanishad there is a striking sentence
which speaks of "That from which all words turn back, together with the mind." That is what we are seeking, and that
is why it is so difficult. Today we are schooled in the language
of reason from the age of five or six. The child begins to be
educated in rational, scientific, mathematical knowledge —
or it may be history or sociology — but always using the rational mind. More and more he thinks the whole world can be
controlled by the rational mind. This is a great illusion, as I
have said, a great ignorance, in the view of all ancient wisdom, because beyond the mind is this hidden spirit, this Atman, this Self. That is what we have to find.

There is a beautiful expression of this in the Chandogya
Upanishad: "There is this City of Brahman, (that is the
body), and in this city there is a shrine, and in that shrine
there is a small lotus, and in that lotus there is a small space,
(*akasa*). Now, what exists within that small space, that is to

be sought, that is to be understood." This is the great discovery of the Upanishads, this inner shrine, this *guha*, or cave of the heart, where the inner meaning of life, of all human existence, is to be found.

The Upanishads have a message for the whole of the western world. We are enclosed in the rational mind, and the reason why thousands of young people are going to India year after year is because they feel imprisoned in this system. It is a prison, eventually: there is something which is being suppressed the whole time. That is why many people go from home and travel to distant parts. They want to get away from the whole system and so they go to India. There they begin to discover this hidden mystery beyond the reason. This is the space which we have to find, the place of this mystery.

We come now to the Katha Upanishad, which shows the way to the heart of the mystery. So far we have been looking at the Brihadaranyaka and the Chandogya, which introduce us to the hidden mystery of Brahman and Atman, and point us to this mystery of our inner being, to the question "Who am I?" A further stage is reached in the Katha Upanishad, which I recommend to anybody who wants to embark on the study of the Upanishads — I don't think there is any better place to begin. It is short, and you need not understand everything in it, but I think you will find that it shows the way to the heart of the mystery.

In it there is the story of a Brahmin who makes a sacrifice which is intended to be a sacrifice of everything he possesses. But instead of offering what is really worthwhile he offers a lot of old cows which "have drunk water, eaten hay, given their milk and are barren." In other words, he offers a lot of useless things in a formal sacrifice. This represents formal religion. Here again, young people today are extremely sensitive to what they consider hypocrisy. They think all religious people are hypocritical. They have elaborate ceremonies and make solemn professions of faith in church, but outside they are no better than others. This is not altogether true, of course, but there is a certain truth in it. Hypocrisy is the vice of religion. It is found in every religion to this day.

So the Katha Upanishad represents this father, this typical Brahmin priest who offers the external sacrifice, but has not made the sacrifice within. He has a son, Nachiketas, who is only a boy, and has learned that his father had promised to give up all that he possessed. The son, therefore, thinking that he also should be offered, says to his father, "Dear Father, to whom will you give me?" He asks this three times, and his father replies in anger, "I will give you to Death." This is like the sacrifice of Abraham in reverse. The son offers himself and the father gives him to Death.

Nachiketas then goes down into the underworld and meets *Yama*, the god of Death. Now, this is a fundamental principle of all religious teaching. If you want to reach your true Self, if you want to find God, you have to die. In the Christian tradition baptism is death. To be baptised is to participate in the death of Christ. The ego has to undergo this death, the ego, which is the *persona*, the mask which we seek to preserve.

So Nachiketas goes down into the world of Death and Death offers him three boons. The first boon Nachiketas asks for is that on his return from death he may be reconciled with his father. This is an important stage in the spiritual life. The seeker has gone out from house and family in search of Truth. He has eventually to return and be reconciled with his past, with the tradition of his family and people. The second boon is that he may know the nature of the fire sacrifice. The fire sacrifice signifies, as has been said, the offering of everything in the Cosmic fire, the fire of life. Every created thing has to be sacrificed, that is, offered to God, if it is to become a source of blessings. The third boon asked is the answer to the question, what lies beyond death? "There is that doubt, when a man is dead; some say he is, others say he is not. This I should like to know, taught by you."

People do everything they can to make this world comfortable, to make people live as long as possible, to make them forget, even in hospital, that death exists. But death is going to come in the end for everybody.

Yama does not want to answer. He says, "This is very difficult. Even the gods doubted about this. Ask me something else. Ask anything you like and I will give it to you, but don't ask about this."

It is a common experience that when you want to find the ultimate truth, to find God, people will offer you anything else — family, friends, possessions, knowledge, power, anything but God.

So Nachiketas goes to Death to try to find the Beyond. Eventually Death gives way and answers him. He begins to speak to him about the Atman, the Self, and he says, "There is the Self of whom many are even unable to hear and whom many even when they hear of Him, do not comprehend."

This is the great problem. Some people cannot even hear of the Self. It has no meaning at all. For many people words like "God" and the "Soul" have lost all meaning. For example, the linguistic analysts in Oxford and elsewhere say that all words apart from those which relate to things which can be scientifically verified are simply meaningless." God," the "soul," "immortality," are words which are simply meaningless. One cannot speak about these things to such people unless they undergo some interior revolution. Something must happen which changes them, or they cannot even hear about these things. Others, even when they hear about them, cannot comprehend. They may feel, "Well, perhaps God exists, perhaps there is a soul, but still it is something very vague, whereas this world is so real." They just push the question aside.

Then Death says, "Wonderful is the man when found who is able to teach Him. Wonderful is he who comprehends Him when taught." We have to have a teacher, we have to find a guru. This is the Hindu tradition. This wisdom comes down from a guru who has had the experience of God. A guru has to have that experience. He doesn't know *about* God; it is not a theory about God, *but an experience of God* in the inner heart. Then only this knowledge can be communicated to another. This is a great lesson for us. We tend to think that one can hand over the Christian faith in a Catechism, but it is of no use unless the inner meaning of it has been grasped. What happens to so many people today is that after leaving school they give up the practice of their faith. People come to our Ashram and tell me, "Until I was fifteen or sixteen, I was a devout Catholic; I used to be a Mass Server, I used to go to Mass regularly, and to Confession, and then when I was sixteen, I gave it all up."

They go out into a secular world, where all these things appear meaningless, and it simply drops away. And why? Because they have learned that faith externally. They have been to Mass, they have learned their Catechism, but they have not discovered God dwelling in their hearts. They have not had an awakening. I believe that Confirmation should be the sacrament of this awakening. When you are about sixteen and you have begun to think for yourself; then you should begin to realize the inner meaning of what you have learned, so that it becomes a personal experience.

In the Hindu tradition the Guru is one who has attained knowledge of God, or Brahman, a knowledge based on experience, and who can communicate this knowledge to his disciple. There is a need of Christian gurus who can not merely teach catechism, but can communicate the knowledge of Christ. This could well be the value of Confirmation — to enable someone to awaken to this knowledge of Christ given through the experience of the Holy Spirit.

Some of these Hindu gurus may be superficial in many ways, but nearly all of them have some kind of inner knowledge. There is the Maharaji who was a boy of sixteen, the founder of the Divine Light Mission; he communicated a certain 'knowledge' to his disciples. I have met several of them. They said he had a certain technique, a certain knowledge, an experiential knowledge which he communicated. That is what people are looking for. They will not accept theories, doctrines, rituals. They want to experience within. It may be a very imperfect experience, but what they want is experience. We should be able to communicate the experience of the Holy Spirit, of Christ within. That is what people are seeking today. This has to be learned from a guru.

The text continues, "That doctrine is not to be obtained by argument. When it is declared by another, then, O dearest, it is easy to understand." That is the nature of faith. Faith is an illumination of the mind. In the Greek church it is called *photismos*, illumination. Faith is a gift of God, a divine illumination, which awakens the mind, and you have to receive it from another. When it is declared by another, then it is easy to understand. "Thou hast obtained it now, now thou art truly a man of resolve."

Now we come to what is to me, one of the most profound sayings in all the Upanishads. We have been through death, we have died in baptism, we have been awakened by faith through the guru, and now he is asking us to go further to discover ourselves. This is what he says: "The wise, who, by means of meditation on his Self, recognizes the Ancient who is difficult to be seen, who has entered into the dark, who is hidden in the cave, who dwells in the abyss as God; he indeed leaves joy and sorrow far behind." This is the experience of contemplation: the experience of God in the darkness. I think we all need to go through that. We may have some experience, some knowledge of God through faith which we learn from a teacher; and then we have got to go on this inner journey into the darkness. That is why it is so difficult, and that is why so many people turn back at that point. They cannot face the darkness, which St John of the Cross called "the dark night of the soul," but which is perhaps better described as the Cloud of Unknowing. It is a venture of faith into the dark. You have to go beyond your mind into that darkness, to find the 'Ancient,' the primeval source of your being, who is "difficult to be seen, who has entered into the dark, who is hidden in the cave, who dwells in the abyss as God." This Self on which you are meditating is the Spirit of God Himself. You have to make that journey into your innermost Self where God is dwelling in the cave of the heart.

But this journey cannot be undertaken by man alone. Therefore the text continues: "This knowledge cannot be gained by the Vedas, nor by understanding, nor by much learning. He whom the Self chooses, by him the Self can be gained." Now this is a doctrine of grace. It is not universal in Hinduism. There are systems which rely entirely on human effort. If you follow the exercises and meditations, you will reach the goal. Many Hindus take that point of view. But the doctrine of grace entered at this period and it has never been lost. And for the more simple Hindu it is quite fundamental. They have some beautiful ideas about grace. For instance, they will say that when a devotee calls on Vishnu in his need, Vishnu will leave his seat in heaven and run to his worshipper to help him.

So this Self cannot be gained by study of the Vedas, or any Scriptures. Simply to study the Scriptures is not enough, though they are necessary; but by studying Scripture you cannot reach the Self. Nor by understanding, nor by much learning. "He whom the Self chooses, by him the Self can be gained." So we have to go beyond the body, beyond the mind, and open ourselves to the hidden mystery of God within and allow this hidden mystery to reveal itself. The Atman, the Brahman, has to reveal himself in the depths of our soul. Only then will we know ourselves. Only then will we come to true self-knowledge. They speak of *Brahmavidya, Atmavidya* — 'knowledge of Brahman,' 'knowledge of the Atman.' That is the supreme knowledge we all seek. In the next talk we will go on to see how this Brahman, this Atman, is also *Purusha*, a 'Person,' whom we need to worship and to love.

The Revelation of the Cosmic Person (Purusha)

Om purnamadah purnamidam
purnat purnam udachyate
Purnasya purnamadaya
purnam eva avashishyate
Om shanti shanti shanti

" "That is full, this is full. From fullness, fullness proceeds. Removing fullness from fullness, fullness alone remains."

This may seem a very mysterious utterance but it has a very deep meaning. Each people has its own particular gifts in the search for God, for truth, for reality. The starting point of the Hindu's search is somewhat different from the Christian's. Revelation for the Christian starts in the Bible, with the idea of a transcendent God and a creation. We in the West tend to think in those terms, but to understand Hindu revelation we have to start from the opposite point of view, that of an immanent God. The three words which express this mystery are, as has been said, Brahman, Atman, and Purusha. Brahman is the word for the inexpressible mystery of Being, of life, of reality, which is manifested in the creation. Atman, which is best translated 'Spirit,' is the manifestation of this inexpressible mystery in the heart of man. And finally, Purusha is the Person. The question I want to raise now is whether this God, this Brahman, this Atman, is a person.

For Christians, God is essentially a person. God in the Old Testament, Yahweh, is a personal God above everything. But with the Hindu Brahman and Atman we don't know, at first, whether a person is referred to or not. The words seem to imply an immanent Presence. The Hindu sage, starting from this world, and from the Divine Presence in the world, is the seer who has seen beyond this world, beyond the world of the senses, beyond the world of human understanding. He has seen 'That.' He sometimes will not give it any other name, just *tat*, 'That.' And then he will say that 'This,' this world which we all experience, is 'That.'

Now, what is the relation between this world and That? We ask that question all the time. What is the relation between Man and God, between this world and God? All sorts of answers are given today. In the fifth century B.C. in India men faced this problem at its deepest level. To my mind they reached the deepest understanding of all.

Purnam adah, purnam idam means " 'That' is God, the infinite Beyond," which is a *purnam*, a 'fullness,' or, as the New Testament calls it, a *pleroma*, a 'fullness of Being.' "This" world which we experience is also a purnam, or fullness. Take the fullness of this world from the fullness of God, and He remains eternally the same. The world neither adds anything to God nor takes anything away.

This is a profound intuition of the relation between "this" world and "That," a relationship which is a perennial problem. All European philosophers have struggled with it. The Indian sages had faced it at this early period, but they have interpreted it in different ways in the course of their history. There are at least three different doctrines in the Hindu tradition with regard to this relationship. This takes us beyond the Upanishads into later philosophical schools of interpretation but I think we should mention them in order to set the Upanishads in the context of the continuing tradition.

The tendency is to say that Hinduism is either monistic or pantheistic. The doctrine of Sankara in the ninth century A.D. was based on the teaching of the Upanishads which were called *Vedanta* — the end of the Vedas, the final stage. But after the Upanishads there came the Bhagavad-Gita which was soon included among the sacred texts of the Vedanta. Then there came the Brahma Sutras or Vedanta Sutras of Badayarana, dating perhaps from the first century A.D., which were the final addition to the canon. All the doctors of Vedanta in the Middle Ages studied and commented upon these three texts. They were called the Triple Foundation of Vedanta.

The Doctors of Vedanta correspond almost exactly with the Christian medieval scholastic theologians in method; Sankara is sometimes called the St Thomas of Hinduism. He is the great orthodox philosopher of the ninth century. He lived in Kerala, South India, and taught the doctrine of *Advaita* — 'non-duality:' there is no duality between God and the world. Sankara was succeeded in the eleventh century by Ramanuja, a theologian who lived in Srirangram, a temple town about twenty miles from our Ashram. Ramanuja taught *Visishtad-vaita*, 'qualified nonduality.' Finally, in the thirteenth century came Madhva who lived in South Canara, in what was later Mysore State. He taught *Dvaita*, 'duality.' They explored all possible relations between God and the world. One said God and the world are not two. Another said that they are not two, but the world qualifies God in some way. The third said that God and the world are two; they are different.

Now, many would think that Madhva's idea of duality is nearest to Christian Doctrine, but in fact the God of Madhva is not really fully transcendent. There is duality but the world and souls are eternal; they do not depend for their existence on the creator. Ramanuja's doctrine is very attractive, because he taught that God is a God of love, and he taught the Doctrine of Grace. The soul turns to God through His grace, and is united with Him in love. That seems very near to Christian belief; but there is also an element of pantheism in Ramanuja. He compared God and the world to the soul and the body. God is the soul, and the whole creation, including human souls, are the body. This is called 'qualified nonduality.' The world in some ways qualifies God, and that is not acceptable from a Christian point of view, yet each of these views points to one aspect of the total reality.

Now we come to Sankara. He is considered the great master. The majority of educated Hindus today are Advaitins, and accept Sankara's basic philosophy. But this can be interpreted in different ways. When I first came to India, I encountered Advaita on every side, especially among professors in the University and among the more educated people. But among them, Advaita, non-duality, is really monism. For them, this world, human beings, and a personal God, are all appearances — what they call 'superimpositions' on the one reality of the Brahman. The one reality is without any differences and distinctions at all. You and I, the table and chairs, the earth and sky, all disappear when we come to full realization — and not only you and I, but also any Personal God disappears. Only the one Brahman, in pure identity, remains. That is monism; Brahman alone is and all the rest is *maya* — illusion. This is very commonly held. Monists will tell you that as long as you are living in this world, in your present state of consciousness, then of course you must recognize you are different from that person, the table, and so forth. But all this is really an illusion, a kind of dream. When you wake up, you will know that there are no differences.

That is one interpretation of Sankara. It is only one school of Vedanta, and a particular interpretation of one school. Very eminent swamis will say, "This is Vedanta, this is Hindu

Doctrine.'' It is not so. It is a particular school, and a particular interpretation. It happens that two Catholic philosophers in India have made a special study of Sankara, De Smet and Sarah Grant. They both took doctorates at a Hindu university, and both were able to affirm that the doctrine of Sankara is much more subtle. It is not pure monism at all. Sankara is much nearer to the view expressed in the verse at the start of this talk: *purnam adah, purnam idam*. Sankara says that this world is neither *sat*, 'being,' nor *asat*, 'not being.' It is something between being and not being. We would say it is becoming. It has a purely relative existence. He compares it to the sun shining into pools of water. There is only one sun, one life, one truth, one reality, and it manifests itself in this, in that, in you, and in me. These are reflections of the one reality. This, I believe, comes very near to the Christian understanding.

De Smet has written an interesting article, ''Can We Have a Christian Advaita?'' I think that we must say that it is possible, because for Christians God and the world are not two. The world does not add anything to God and it does not take anything away from God. Therefore they do not exist in the same kind of way. St Thomas Aquinas is clear about this: the world has a purely relative reality. That, I think, is what Sankara is trying to say. This world, and you and I, are real, but with a completely relative reality.

This world, without Brahman, is pure illusion. It is nothing. But this world in Brahman has relative reality. That is a genuine advaita which Christians can accept. It comes very close to the Hebrew conception of man as the image of God. The Greek fathers took this to mean that each man, each person, is like a mirror reflecting God. You and I are mirrors, each reflecting God in a unique way. Yet there is only one God shining in you, shining in me. Sin distorts the mirror and obscures the light. When the mirror is purified and the light shines, then each of us perfectly reflects God. In the beatific vision each human being is a pure reflection of the one light shining uniquely in each one. This would be a Christian interpretation of advaita, non-duality.

To come back to the Upanishads: in the Katha Upanishad we have a text which says, "There are these two drinking their reward in the world of their own works, entered into the cave of the heart, dwelling on the highest summit. Those who know Brahman call them light and shade." In the previous talk, we saw how in the depths of the heart there is the indwelling presence of the Atman, the Spirit of God.

Here the question is, what is the relation between my spirit and the Spirit of God? In Hindu terms the words are *jivatman*, 'the individual soul,' and *Paramatman*, 'the Supreme Spirit.' That is the question. It has been answered differently by different doctors and it is still disputed. The Svestasvatara Upanishad gives us a further clue when it says, "There are two birds, inseparable friends, clinging to the same tree. One of them eats the sweet fruit, the other looks on without eating." Then it explains, "On the same tree, man sits grieving, immersed in the world, bewildered by his own impotence." He is called *anisa*, 'without power,' in contrast to *Isa*, the Lord, who is with power. "But when he sees the other, the Lord, contented, and knows His glory, then his grief passes away."

So at this stage we have a teaching that there are two birds, the individual soul, and the Supreme Spirit; and there is the world. When the soul looks down into the world and gets immersed and involved in it, it gets bewildered and confused and loses itself. That is what the Christian means by original sin, the turning away from God and being absorbed in the world. But when it looks up and sees the Lord within, the Paramatman, the Supreme Spirit, then its grief passes away. The two, the individual spirit and the Supreme Spirit, meet in the heart. The whole question is whether we turn in our heart towards God and receive this fullness, this *purnam*, life and being, or whether we turn away from God, get immersed in the world, and lose ourselves. It is the perennial choice between God and the world.

Let us look now into the question, "Who is the Lord?" He has been called the Paramatman, the Supreme Spirit, and as we have seen, He is one with the Supreme Brahman. Atman and Brahman are one; Brahman is his name when manifested in the whole creation, Atman when manifested in the human being. But who is this Lord, this person? Let us go back to the Rig-Veda, to a remarkable text from the tenth book of the Rig-Veda which speaks of a *Purusha. Purusha* means 'man,' the 'cosmic man,' or, better, the 'cosmic person.' When we think of man, we tend to think man is a little person on this earth, very limited, with a great universe of innumerable galaxies beyond him. We limit him to that. But in the ancient vision of the world man embraced the whole creation, as in fact he does: the creation is within us. Our mind has the capacity to embrace the whole creation. Cosmic man, this Purusha, is said to be beyond the whole creation: "A thousand heads has Purusha. A thousand eyes, a thousand feet, on every side he pervades the earth."

A thousand heads, a thousand eyes, a thousand feet signifies that the cosmic man, the cosmic person, is present in you and me and every person. Thousand is a number of fullness. He is manifest in the one Person; he is manifest in all persons. Each of us is a little Purusha, and there is the one great Purusha who embraces us all.

Then it says, "This Purusha is all that has been and all that will be. He encompasses the whole creation. He is the Lord of immortality. Mighty is his greatness." And then there is the statement, "One-fourth of Him is here on earth, three-fourths are above in heaven." It is very crude in a way, dividing into fourths, but one can see the meaning. One-fourth is immanent on earth, manifesting in you and me, three-fourths are the dimension of his being above in heaven. This is the cosmic man, the cosmic person.

A still more remarkable insight is that creation comes from the sacrifice of Purusha. At the beginning of time Purusha is sacrificed and his limbs are scattered over the world. In the ritual sacrifice Purusha is gathered together and becomes one again. This has a profound relationship to the conception of Adam and the Son of Man. As St Augustine said, "Adam, at his fall, was scattered over all the earth." Man was once one, one with nature, one with himself, one with God. And then when he fell he was scattered and divided. The atonement means that God comes into this divided universe and gathers those scattered pieces together and in his sacrifice reunites mankind. He brings all these persons together in his Person. Another wonderful text of St Augustine says, "In the end there will be *unus Christus amans seipsum* — One Christ, loving himself in all his members."

We can see in this conception in the Vedas of a Cosmic Person through whose sacrifice the world comes into being a profound analogy with the Biblical concept of Christ as the "Lamb who was slain before the foundation of the world," the cosmic man by whose sacrifice the world is sustained.

Jesus called himself the Son of Man. It seemed to have been the one title that he felt most meaningful. It is one of those phrases which has many meanings. It can mean simply "man." In Ezekiel God says, "Son of Man, stand on your feet," or again, in the Psalm it says, "What is Man that thou art mindful of him, or the Son of Man, that thou visitist him?" It is simply a synonym. Son of Man is Man. This Son of Man was at the beginning. He is the "Adam," the man who in St Luke's Gospel is said to be the Son of God, the man who comes from God. So there is the Adam, the Man at the beginning. But there is also the Son of Man who is to come in the clouds of heaven at the end of time, and there is no doubt that in Jesus' mind that figure was a figure of himself. At the trial, in the presence of Caiaphas, the high priest, Jesus said, "You shall see the Son of Man coming on the clouds of heaven." He identified himself as the Son of Man spoken of by Daniel. This man was at the beginning, this man will come at the end of time; and this man, this Adam, is present now in each individual man. So there we have a Christian Doctrine of the Purusha, the primeval Man.

In India there is today an attempt to create an Indian Christian Theology. We seek to express our Christian faith in the language of the Vedanta as the Greek Fathers expressed it in the language of Plato and Aristotle. Purusha will be one of the key words in an Indian Christian Theology. Advaita would be another.

In the Katha Upanishad, which as has been mentioned is one of the short Upanishads from about the fifth century B.C., there is a very interesting description of Man. He is compared to a chariot, an ancient symbol. It comes in Plato: the chariot is the body, and the man seated in the chariot is the soul. In this Upanishad it is somewhat more elaborated: "Know the Self, the Atman as seated in the chariot, the body as the chariot, the intellect, the *buddhi*, as the charioteer, and the mind, the *manas*, as the reins. The senses they call the horses, the objects of the senses, their roads. When the highest Self is in union with the body, the senses, and the mind, then the wise call him the Enjoyer."

Human nature is so constructed that through our senses we journey on the roads of this material world. Above the senses is the manas. Manas comes from the root *ma*, meaning 'to measure.' We use the same root when we speak of the moon. The moon measures time. And the root of *mens*, or 'mind,' is probably the same. So it is the measuring mind; the rational, scientific mind — which most people today think is the full extent of the human mind. Manas is the lower mind. But above the manas is the buddhi, and *buddhi* comes from the root which means 'to enlighten.' The Buddha is the Enlightened One. The buddhi is that higher intelligence which illumines the manas, the mind, and receives its light from above, from the Spirit beyond. The buddhi is fundamental, but it no longer has any place in most European philosophy; we think in terms of the senses and the mind. But beyond the mind is the buddhi. That is our point of transcendence, of going beyond. To reach the buddhi is the purpose of all meditation. We have to get beyond the manas, which is the organ of the ego, the ''I,'' and to open ourselves to transcendence.

St Thomas distinguished the *intellectus* and the *ratio*. Ratio is the lower mind, the reasoning mind, which works through the senses. Intellectus is the pure intelligence which knows first principles and is able to know God. In Sanskrit that is the buddhi.

Beyond the buddhi is the *Mahat*, the 'the Great Self.' That is the cosmic order, and that is something of which we have almost lost any conception today. Beyond the individual mind and the individual intelligence — the spirit of man — there is the cosmic order, the world of the angels. We have forgotten this world of the angels. St Thomas said the human intelligence is the lowest level of intelligence; beyond man are the angels, and beyond the angels are the archangels, then the thrones, dominations, virtues, princedoms, powers, and finally the seraphim and the cherubim. Then we come to God beyond all. These are all levels of consciousness. The western mind since the seventeenth century has confined itself almost exclusively to the lowest levels of consciousness and has rejected all these higher levels. Today people are discovering them; they speak of a new consciousness which is beginning to emerge. In the Hindu tradition it has been understood from the beginning that there are many levels of consciousness. We need to go beyond the manas and the buddhi to the cosmic consciousness, the mahat; this is the world of the angels and the 'gods,' the cosmic powers. But beyond the mahat is the unmanifest, and that again is a deeper level of consciousness. Before anything comes into manifestation in this world, either through the senses or through the mind, it is unmanifest in God. Christians would say that the whole creation comes into being originally in the Word of God. Before there was any time the whole creation exists potentially in this Word. Meister Eckhart said, "God only speaks one Word, and in that Word the whole creation comes into being." You and I and every event in space and time exist potentially in that one Word. The whole creation exists in its unmanifest state in the one Word.

In the Katha Upanishad it says, "Beyond the unmanifest, the *avyakta*, is the Purusha, and beyond the Purusha there is nothing. That is the goal, that is the highest end." This, then, is the course of the ascent of man through the senses and through the mind, to the buddhi, to the cosmic order, the cosmic consciousness, to the unmanifest beyond, and finally, to Purusha himself, the Person, the Word of God. That is the path of ascent to God.

Then it says — and in this context we have to remember that Brahman, Atman and Purusha can all be used of the same Being, the same mystery, the Word of God — "That Atman is hidden in all beings and does not shine forth." One never loses touch with this world as one ascends to the Purusha beyond the whole creation, for He is present in this table, in this room, in me, in you. He is hidden in everything, but he does not shine forth. We have to discover him hidden everywhere. "He is seen by the subtle seers, through their sharp and subtle intellect."

The Upanishad now shows the path of meditation as the

way to reach this Being, and this is the process: "A wise man should keep down speech in mind." Speech is the movement by which we go out of ourselves to communicate to another. When one begins to meditate one has to withdraw from others. It is a process: one goes out again afterward, but one has to begin by withdrawing, keeping down speech in the mind, or *manas*. And then, one must keep the mind within the 'Self which is knowledge,' that is, in the buddhi. Meditation consists in learning to control the mind, for thoughts keep wandering here and there, and one is thinking about this and that. To control that movement of the mind is the first principle of Yoga. The Yoga Sutras of Patanjali begin: "Yoga is the cessation of the movements of the mind." Many people today are trying to learn how to stop the mind. When the mind, or *manas*, stops, then the light of the intellect begins to shine. The mind is ordinarily scattered and dissipated. But gather the mind into one and then the pure light shines in the mirror which is oneself. So keep the mind, the manas, within the Self which is knowledge, and the buddhi, the intellect, within the 'Self which is the Great,' the Mahat, the Cosmic Order, the world of the gods. We have to open ourselves to the world of the angels and the spirits. St Gregory of Nyssa, who was the greatest mystical theologian in the early church, conceived the illuminative way as the contemplation of the world of the angels, which really means the world of Divine Providence working through the angels, the spiritual powers in creation, in humanity, and in the Church. The illuminative way is the contemplation of the Mahat, the Cosmic Order.

In the final stage, as the Katha Upanishad says, "He should keep that, the Self which is the Great, within the Self which is peace." That is the peace which passes understanding, the *Shanta-Atman*, the 'Self of Peace.' With this we come to the final stage, when we pass beyond phenomena, beyond all dualities, to the One Self, who is in all.

The Cosmic Revelation

This is a doctrine which is also a discipline. In all Oriental teaching we must never separate the doctrine from the discipline, Vedanta from Yoga — they go together. It is no good learning about these things unless we learn to experience within ourselves the reality which is there in each one of us. The Shanta-Atman is in each one of us. In the midst of the cities, in the noise of the streets and in the excitement of life, there is a hidden peace, and it is in each one of us. This is the Shanta-Atman.

Then comes a wonderful phrase which is written over the gates of Sivananda Ashram in Rishikesh: "Awake! Arise! Having obtained your boons, be Enlightened!" The buddhi is the faculty through which illumination comes. There is no separation as we pass from the senses to the mind, to the buddhi, to the whole cosmic order, through the Unmanifest, till we reach to the Person of God. That Person is present in the senses, in the mind, in the buddhi, and in the mahat, the cosmic order. He pervades the whole and we can find Him everywhere in everything, and in one another.

Now we reach a verse which exactly defines the characteristic movement of Hindu thought:

"The Self existent (that is the Creator) pierced the openings of the senses, so that they turn outwards. Therefore, man looks outwards, not into himself." We experience this today more than at any other time: we all look outwards into the world around us. "But one wise man, desiring immortality, looked within and found the Self." That is what took place in India during the fifth century B.C. A wise man looked within and discovered the hidden presence, the Atman, the Spirit within the heart.

Let us go from the Katha Upanishad to the great revelation of the personal God in the Svetasvatara Upanishad. This is a somewhat later Upanishad, perhaps of the third century, B.C. It is sometimes not included in the classical Upanishads, but it is most profound, and from our point of view it is the most important. It is called a Theistic Upanishad, and nowhere in the Upanishads is the doctrine of a personal God portrayed with such extraordinary power. To me it has been a great enrichment to study this Upanishad. It is fascinating to watch the human mind discover a personal God from its own experience of the world. So many people in our own time are awakening to the fact of a personal God.

The text speaks of "The Brahma-students . . ." that is, the Brahmacharis. The word *brahmachari* signifies properly 'moving in Brahman' and refers to a student who is engaged in the study of the Vedas, which communicate the Knowledge of Brahman. As the student observed celibacy during this period of study, brahmachari came to signify celibacy. But it has a much wider meaning, which comes very close to the Benedictine idea of 'seeking God.'

The Brahma-students say, "Is Brahman the cause? Whence are we born? Whereby do we live? Whither do we go? Oh you who know Brahman, tell us at whose command we abide, whether in pain or in pleasure?" These are questions which human beings still ask. Where do we come from? How do we live? Where are we going? Millions are asking these questions today and do not know the answers.

Then the text suggests all the possible answers. These are all answers which have been given by modern philosophers. "Should time, or nature, or necessity, or chance, or the elements be considered the cause?" How many modern philosophers and scientists have said that time or nature or necessity are the cause? The French biologist, Jacques Monod, wrote a famous book not very long ago, saying the whole universe could be explained in terms of chance and necessity.

In India in the third century B.C. they had already considered this possibility and had rejected it. To the question,

"Is it chance or necessity which is the cause of the world?" the Upanishad answers: "The sages devoted to the Yoga of meditation have seen the power of God himself hidden in his own qualities, He being one rules over all these causes, time and the rest." The answer is given, it is to be noticed, not as the outcome of merely scientific or philosophical knowledge, but of the Yoga of meditation — that is, from the deeper centre of consciousness which is discovered in meditation. And it is found in the *devatmasakti*, the 'power,' *sakti*; of the 'Self,' *atman*; of 'God,' *deva*. The Self or Spirit of God is the immanent presence of God in creation. Here the seer has penetrated beyond the external phenomenon to the reality, the truth, behind the phenomenon — the Power of God.

This power of God is what is called the Brahman, the reality behind all phenomena. Of this it is said: "Those who have known beyond this (world) the High Brahman, the Vast, hidden in the bodies of all creatures and alone enveloping all things as the Lord, they become immortal." Here we have the clearest insight into the thought of the Upanishads. This Brahman, the Power of God, is hidden in all creatures, but at the same time 'envelops them' — it is both immanent and transcendent, it is also the Lord, the personal God. It is now clear that the Brahman, the immanent presence in all things, and the Atman, the Spirit of God in man, are both one with the Lord, the Purusha, the personal God. And this is not merely a speculative theory but a fact of experience. This is beautifully expressed in a *sloka* which says: "When by the real nature of the Atman he sees as by a lamp the real nature of Brahman, then having known the one eternal God, who is beyond all natures, he is freed from bondage." This is a knowledge of the Self, that is, of the human being at the deepest level of consciousness, which gives an insight into the real nature of being and leads to the knowledge of the 'eternal God,' the Personal God.

The Revelation of the Cosmic Person

We come now to a further insight. This Brahman, this Atman, which reveals itself as a Personal God can only be known by 'grace.' "The Self smaller than the small and greater than the great is hidden in the heart of the creature. A man who has left all grief behind sees the majesty of the Lord by the grace of the Creator." One sometimes hears it said that Hinduism knows nothing of divine grace. A passage such as this, which can be paralleled in other Upanishads, shows the falsity of this view. There are Hindu systems of philosophy which do not recognise the presence of grace, but the doctrine is firmly rooted in the most ancient tradition of the Vedas.

It is to be noticed that all along the Upanishads start from the immanence of God in creation. It is the 'power of God hidden in nature' with which the Upanishads are concerned, and this differentiates them from the typical Judeo-Christian tradition, which always starts from the transcendence of God. But at the same time the Hindu comes to recognise the transcendence of God. This is particularly true of the Svetasvatara Upanishad. Nowhere else does one find such a clear affirmation of the absolute transcendence of the one supreme personal God. Of his unity, it declares emphatically:

"There is one Rudra only, they do not allow a second and he rules all the worlds by his power." Then it goes on to say:

"He is the one God, hidden in all beings, all-pervading, the Self within all beings, watching over the world, the witness, the knower, the only one, beyond the constituents of nature." Finally, the appeal is made in words which make us think of the Hebrew prophets:

"Let us know that supreme great Lord of lords, the supreme God of gods, the supreme Ruler of rulers, the adorable, the transcendent, the Lord of the universe." We could not have a more clear monotheism than this, and this is a peak point in Hinduism. I do not want to suggest that all Hin-

83

dus are monotheists. There are Hindus who are practically atheists, others who are agnostics, others who are fatalists, and still others who are monists. But in the Hindu sacred texts themselves there is this witness to an experience of God as both pervading the universe, dwelling in the heart, and as a Person, as the Lord beyond all lords, beyond all gods, beyond all the powers of this world, to be worshipped and adored.

"He is the one God hidden in all beings, all pervading, the Self within all beings." He is my inner Self. We must understand that the spirit of man is a dynamic point; at that point of the spirit I am open to the spirit of God. Karl Rahner says somewhere that, "Man is constituted by his capacity for Self-transcendence." We are not fully human until we transcend our human state. We are made for God. And the Spirit is that point where the human spirit meets the Spirit of God. When we respond to His grace we open on the divine, and when we resist that grace, then we fall from God. We fall from that point of the spirit to the psyche, the soul with all its faculties and powers; then we become subject to the powers of this world, the demonic powers as well as all the other powers. But at the point of the spirit is the Self within all beings. At the still point within my spirit meets the Spirit of God, "watching over all works, dwelling in all beings, the Witness, the Knower, the only One, free from qualities." The qualities are the constituents of this world — but He is free from all these qualities — one alone, beyond everything.

There is a beautiful phrase which comes in more than one Upanishad where it says of the world beyond, "The sun does not shine there, nor the moon nor the stars nor these lightnings, much less this earthly fire. When He shines, everything shines after Him, by His light all this is enlightened." This reminds us of the words of the Revelation of St John: "The city has no need of sun or moon to shine upon it, for the glory of God is its light." It is a wonderful intuition of the mystery of creation.

"Seeking for liberation I go for refuge to that God who is the light of His own thoughts." The dynamism of this Upanishad is in this search for liberation: to be liberated from bondage to all the psychological mechanisms which we know bind us to our own ego; liberation is to be set free from all this and to open upon the infinite world of the spirit. That is what is behind these speculations. It is never speculation for the sake of speculation, never pure philosophy. It is a mystical theology. Many of us think today that Christian theology has to become a mystical theology once again. Henri De Lubac, a great friend of one of the founders of our ashram, Jules Monchanin, once wrote to him, "Your task is to rethink everything in terms of theology, and theology in terms of mysticism." Many feel today that that is what the Church needs. Christian theology has become a scientific, philosophical, theological system, but it has lost that dimension of contemplative wisdom which St Thomas Aquinas and Augustine and all the Fathers had. We want to recover this dynamism using science, and philosophy, and theology, as means, not ends, to bring us to liberation, to the freedom within. When we are open to God, and therefore open to man, we attain our full freedom. "Seeking for freedom, for liberation, I go for refuge to that God who is the light of His own thoughts." Then the text says, "Through the power of his penance, and through the grace of God, has the wise Svetasvatara truly proclaimed Brahman." How did he reach this knowledge of the Brahman? "By his *Tapas.*" Tapas is effort, discipline, control. But he adds, "and by the grace of God." Without the grace of God, one will never reach this depth of understanding.

Finally the text says, "This highest mystery of the Vedanta, delivered in a former age, should not be given to one whose passions have not been subdued, nor to one who is not a son or a pupil.'' This knowledge is not given to a person who is not prepared for it. But, "If these truths have been told to a high-minded man who feels the highest devotion for God, and for his Guru as for God, then they will shine forth, then they will shine forth, indeed.'' When we approach this with the right mind, with devotion, then the truth shines in our minds. We are awakened, we are Enlightened.

Bhagavad-Gita

We enter upon a new era with the Bhagavad-Gita, "The Song of the Lord." The Vedic Age extends from the Rig-Veda, about 1500 B.C., to the Upanishads upon which we have been meditating, about 500 B.C. Then begins a new age when the Aryan religion began to extend through India and met the Dravidian, the indigenous religion. At this stage the great epics came into being, the Ramayana, the story of Rama, and the Mahabharata, the story of the great war between the sons of Bharat. The Bhagavad-Gita belongs not to the Vedic Age, but to the epic. It was inserted into the great epic, the Mahabharata, perhaps about 300-200 B.C.

The Bhagavad-Gita represents a new spirituality and is a decisive moment in the history of India and of Indian spirituality. In the Upanishads the aim was to seek for knowledge of Brahman, or knowledge of the Atman. Normally it was expected one would have to lead an ascetic life, which meant becoming a Sannyasi, a renunciate. One had to spend time in meditation, and in *sadhana*, 'spiritual practice.' Only then could one expect to reach a state of union with God.

In the Bhagavad-Gita there developed devotion to a personal God, a *Bhagavan*, a 'Lord.' No one knows exactly how it came into being. It is one of those spontaneous movements of the spirit. Devotion to a personal God had been present in the Vedas in a certain way. In the period of the Upanishads it is of much less importance. But now it surges up: it is concerned partly with Shiva and partly with Vishnu as the manifestations of the Supreme God. It is strange that among the great gods of the Vedas, Indra, the king of the gods, is not worshipped in today's India. And other names for God, such as *Prajapati*, the 'Lord of creation,' and *Visva Karma*, the 'Almighty,' have practically disappeared. Even Brahma, a masculine name for the Creator God, becomes a vague figure. But Vishnu and Shiva have become the figures of the Supreme God. Most Hindus today are either Vaishnavites or Shaivites, worshippers of Vishnu or Shiva, and for them Vishnu or Shiva is the name for the Supreme, for Brahman, the absolute reality. In the Mahabharata it is Vishnu who descends upon earth to take the form of Krishna, as an *avatara*, which means literally a 'descent' of God.

The first thing, then, in this new age of spirituality is devotion to a personal God. That means that the worship of God, union with God, is laid open to everyone — to the householder as well as the Sannyasi. That is why the Bhagavad-Gita has become the most popular religious book in India. Many of India's modern leaders, from Mahatma Ghandi onwards, have written commentaries on the Gita. It is a kind of compendium of the religious genius of India. De Smet, one of the best Catholic scholars in India, has shown how many different streams of tradition converge on the Gita, making it a wonderful synthesis of the whole tradition. It draws on the Vedic tradition, particularly on the Upanishads — it really is a kind of Upanishad itself — and it draws on the Buddhist tradition as well. The word Nirvana, for instance, a distinctly Buddhist word, comes into the Bhagavad-Gita, though it is given a slightly new meaning. It is influenced also to some extent by the Jain tradition. Mahavira, the founder of the Jains, was a predecessor of Buddha. In about the sixth century B.C. he established a very ascetic religion with an emphasis on *ahimsa*, non-violence, which has had a profound effect on all Indian spirituality. The Bhagavad-Gita also draws on the *darshanas*, early Indian systems of philosophy, particularly the Samkhya and the Yoga.

The Samkhya philosophy is the original metaphysic of India. Its principal feature is that all creation is seen to rest on two principles, *Purusha* and *Prakriti*. *Purusha* is Person, the Spirit, consciousness, and is masculine. *Prakriti* is nature, matter, and is feminine. It is interesting that in the Indian tradition the woman is the principle of action, the man, of contemplation. The man looks on, the woman does the work. The whole creation is understood as the union of Purusha and Prakriti, of the male and the female.

You will sometimes find European and Christian scholars being scandalised by the sexual symbolism which runs all through Hinduism. This symbolism is, in fact, deeply significant. It holds that God has so created the world that everything is a play of the union of the male and the female, of the active and passive principles. This pervades creation. Everyone and everything has to find this unity of the male and the female. Every woman has to find her unity, or oneness with the male, and every male a oneness with the female. This is the mystery of creation, which forms the basis of the doctrine of the Samkhya.

Yoga, in the early system, is the art of first separating and then uniting Purusha and Prakriti. It is the art of uniting in oneself the male and the female aspect, the conscious and the unconscious, spirit and matter, so as to bring the duality within our nature into unity.

So the Bhagavad-Gita draws on the Vedic tradition and the Upanishads; it draws on the Jain and Buddhist traditions; it draws on the Samkhya and the Yoga traditions; and it draws on the doctrine of *karma*.

Karma means action, the theory of karma is that every action has an inevitable reaction. This works through the whole world of nature and humanity. Every action we do has an inevitable consequence. A good action has a good consequence and an evil action has an evil consequence. We are always suffering or enjoying the effects of our actions. This is the basis of the doctrine of rebirth: you are born in a particular way in this world because of your actions, your karma, in a previous birth. If you are suffering now, it is because you did evil actions in the past. This can become very crude and fatalistic, but it can also be meaningful. It can come very near to the Christian conception of original sin; this depends on how it is interpreted. The Bhagavad-Gita introduces a very profound understanding of what karma really means.

The Gita is therefore a kind of compendium of Indian wisdom. It is a very small book, eighteen chapters only, and not difficult to read. There is a very convenient edition in the Penguin Classics, translated by Mascaro, with an excellent introduction. If anybody wants to start the study of Hinduism I always recommend beginning with the Bhagavad-Gita and then working out from that.

The Gita is part of the epic poem, the Mahabharata, which is the longest poem in the world. It tells the story of the Pandyas and the Kauravas. The Pandyas are five brothers who have the right to the throne, but the throne has been usurped by King Dhritarashtra of the Kauravas and his son Duryodhana. The Pandyas were condemned to go into exile as a result of losing a game of dice. Then, on their return from exile, they claim their right to the throne again, but get no satisfactory response. This leads to the Mahabharata, the great war. The Bhagavad-Gita was inserted into the poem of the Mahabharata at a point where the two armies were about to join battle, and Arjuna, one of the heroes of the Pandyas, was seated in his chariot, facing the enemy. He feels he cannot fight the battle. He sees opposite him the Kauravas, who are his own relations and friends; he sees his guru, his teacher, and his grandfather. So he lays down his arms in despair. This has been understood as a symbol of man faced with the battle of life.

The symbolism is instructive. Dhritarashtra is a blind king who has usurped the throne. He stands for the ego, the false self, the persona, which has usurped the throne of our being. He has a hundred sons. They are all the passions and desires which flow from the ego. The ego always wants more; this is the basis of the consumer society which we have today, in which the desires of the ego are continually advertised and encouraged. Dhritarashtra, then, is the blind Self which has endless desires and appetites. The Pandyas as the rightful owners of the throne are the true Self. They are trying to recover the throne, that is, to restore the spirit to its proper place.

The Gita again uses the symbol of the chariot which we mentioned earlier. The body is the chariot, Arjuna is the soul of man seated in the chariot of the body, and the charioteer is Krishna, the Lord, who has come to instruct and guide the soul. The whole of the Bhagavad-Gita is Krishna's discourse to Arjuna. It is the spirit of God speaking to the spirit of man and teaching him how to conduct his life. That is why it is such a practical book. The message of the Gita is that Arjuna must fight the battle. He lays down his arms and says, "I will not fight. I cannot face life." But Krishna comes and counsels him and teaches him how to fight this battle of life while remaining united with God throughout.

Mahatma Gandhi, although he was deeply influenced by the gospel, really lived by the Bhagavad-Gita. He once said that in all the crises of his life and in all the problems he had to face he found consolation, strength and guidance in the Gita. That is why it has become the great manual of spirituality for the people of India, and can become a manual of spiritual guidance for the West. It has a universal message.

So much, then, for the preliminaries. The Gita is divided into three parts. The first six books are concerned with karma yoga, the yoga of action; the next six books with bhakti yoga, the yoga of love, and the last six with jnana yoga, the yoga of wisdom. These themes interweave with one another, but basically that is the pattern. We find in the first six chapters the most perfect guidance as to how to reach that 'knowledge of God,' that *Brahmavidya*, that 'knowledge of the Self,' that *Atmavidya*, which we are considering in the Upanishads, while yet engaged in the battle of life. I think this is something which we need above everything today: how to face all the demands of life today while retaining the inner awareness of the Spirit of God within, of the Lord dwelling in the heart.

The Gita gives practical guidance as to how this can be done. It shows how work, which includes all action in the world, can become not an obstacle, but a means of union with God. The earlier tradition was that all karma, all work, binds you. Even good work binds you. Your good works attach you to this and to that, and you are bound by the world and cannot escape. Therefore the tradition has been to give up all karma, all work. The Jains took that principle to an extreme. They believe that every kind of action, every karma, adds some impurity to the soul. They attempted therefore gradually to separate themselves from the world and from all activity. Eventually, they retired to a cave until the time was ripe and then they simply allowed the body to drop off. The Jains often starved themselves to death — they just surrendered the body. That was an extreme development of the doctrine of karma.

The Gita has something quite different to say. The Gita says that all work which has a selfish end is binding, and its consequences are inescapable. But all work which is done with an unselfish purpose and in the service of others not only does not bind, but is a means of union with God. There are four principles for this kind of work. The first one is that all work should be done without seeking a reward. "Do not seek the fruit of your actions." So Krishna says, "Set thy heart upon thy work, but never on its reward. Work not for the reward but never cease to do thy work." So you see, it is a gospel of action. This is necessary today. I think that many Christians today are trying to find a way in which they can be engaged in action, in work, in service, while yet making this a means of union with God. The first condition is to do the work, but not to seek the reward, because seeking a reward means that you are putting your ego into your work. Work which starts from the ego — which is the false self, the persona, the mask — all such work will be impure and will bind you. Even work which appears to be good and really is good — for instance the work of a person who cares for the sick, or teaches in a school or college — will be corrupted if the ego goes into the work. Everybody knows that there are people who are extremely capable and manage things wonderfully, but everything must be done as they want it done. They are impossible to live with. Such work can never really be as effective as it should be.

It is the ego which spoils the work. Therefore you have to do your work without looking for reward. You may be given a certain work to do, maybe the charge of a school or hospital or other social work, and after some time you have built up quite a good organisation. You feel some satisfaction in your work, and then you are removed. It may be that the whole thing then goes to pieces. Here you must reflect that you received your work from God, and you must leave the fruit of your work to God. You do not allow yourself to be disturbed. A test of whether your ego is in the work is: when the work fails, or when you have to abandon it, you get extremely depressed or upset. Or again if the work succeeds and does well, you become extremely pleased with yourself. This is a sign that your ego is involved in the work.

One may relinquish the work with sorrow and with pain, but still it must be with total self-surrender. St Ignatius of Loyola was once asked what he would do if the Pope abolished the Society of Jesus (as he did later on) and his answer was, "After half an hour of meditation, I would accept it with complete tranquility." That is how, I think, one ought to accept to do one's work. That is work done without seeking a reward.

The Gita then goes on to say, "Do thy work in the peace of Yoga and free from selfish desires, and be not moved in success or in failure. Yoga is evenness of mind." The Sanskrit is *samatva* — 'sameness.' The goal is to be the same in good or evil, in pleasure or pain, in success or in failure, in honour or dishonour, and to keep that evenness of mind. You suffer, but you do not give way to the suffering. You have inner balance, a harmony of mind. This then is the first condition, not to seek the fruit of one's work.

Here, I think, it is very important to emphasize that this does not mean a kind of indifference to the work which one does. One has to do the work with one's whole heart and soul. One is doing the work for God, but leaving the result to God. It means that the work must be done with detachment. Attachment means that the ego has entered into the work: you are attached to the work and then you are bound by it. When you are detached you do the work and you put your heart into it but you are not bound by it. You are able to let it go when the time comes.

This doctrine of detachment is, I feel, the essential teaching of the gospel also. We must distinguish it from any kind of repression or suppression. In the Christian tradition there exists a rather dangerous tradition from the fathers of the desert

Bhagavad-Gita

of a suppression of the desires, of the passions, of the senses and of the imagination. For those who are strong that may be a way of transformation, and for many thousands of saints it has been the way. But for people today, generally speaking, I think it is nearly always disastrous. It creates a duality. You suppress something in your nature which keeps coming back.

On the other hand, Yoga is never a method of suppression. It is an inner control. You accept the world of the senses. The Gita puts it very well in one passage. It speaks of "the soul that moves in the world of the senses and yet keeps the senses in harmony, free from attraction and aversion." The meaning is that you can enjoy everything in the world. You can enjoy your food and your drink, you can enjoy sex and love, you can enjoy business and activity and whatever comes to you, but it must be enjoyed with fundamental detachment. You are not attached to yourself, to your ego, while you enjoy these things. I think that is also true of an artist of any kind, a dancer, or a musician, or a poet; there has to be a certain detachment. If his ego goes into anything he does it spoils his work.

Another saying in the Gita is: Yoga is "wisdom in work," or "skill in action." Yoga is skill in action. It means that you are so perfectly harmonised — your senses, your feelings, your mind, your heart — that you can act spontaneously, freely. It is to attain an inner freedom and not be the victim of suppressed feelings. This is extremely important, because so many of us have suffered from the suppression of the feelings, of the senses, of the passions, and of sex. This results in psychological maladjustment, and it is very difficult to be free from it. But Yoga is never a suppression of that kind. It is "skill in action."

There is a beautiful story told in the Chinese tradition which shows the ideal of Yoga. There was said to be a Chinese cook who cut up meat with an axe, and the axe always kept its fine edge because he always cut the meat up with absolute precision. He never had to sharpen the blade because he never hit on a bone or anything, he went cleanly between the joints at every point. It was such a marvellous performance that the Emperor came to see this cook cut up the meat. He asked him how he did it, and he said "I first meditate on the Tao." The Tao is the order, the rhythm of the universe. "I put myself in harmony with the Tao, and then I cut up the meat." When you do anything you must first put yourself in harmony with creation, which ultimately means, with God. When you have attained this inner harmony then in the light of that inner harmony your action becomes perfect, like that of an animal in its natural state. An animal is perfectly attuned.

I often think of the mongoose in India. The mongoose can kill a snake, but it has to know exactly when to strike so as not to allow the snake to strike first. This is a perfect example of "skill in action." So it is with the dancer, or any musician or artist: he has a skill in action which is due to this Yoga, this inner harmony. He has freed himself from his ego and he is responding now to the rhythm of nature, he has become harmonized. That, as I said, is the first condition; not seeking a reward, being free from the ego.

The next condition is that everything you do has to be offered in sacrifice. This, of course, is very familiar to Catholics. They are accustomed to offer all the actions of the day in the Mass, in union with Christ. But it is a universal belief that every action of every kind should be offered in sacrifice. I mentioned how eating, drinking, bathing, walking, and taking a journey are all sacred actions in Hinduism. Everything has to be offered. Then you act from the spirit of the universe, from the cosmic order. Then your action is good and has the right effect.

When you sin you withdraw your action from the cosmic

order. You act from your own ego, from your limited self; then you put yourself in opposition to the cosmic order and you create conflict wherever you go. So the Gita says, "Thus spoke the Lord of Creation when he made both man and sacrifice. By sacrifice thou shalt multiply and obtain all thy desires. By sacrifice thou shalt honour the gods, the gods will then love thee and thus, in harmony with them, thou shalt attain the supreme good. So pleased with thy sacrifice, the gods will grant thee all thy desires. Only a thief would enjoy their gifts and not offer them in sacrifice." To take anything, to take a glass of water without offering sacrifice, is to be a thief. The water does not belong to you. You are taking something which belongs to God and you are appropriating it for yourself. That is sin. On the other hand, to take a glass of water in thanksgiving and joy is to make it an act of sacrifice and of worship which brings fulfillment for yourself and for others. Everything should be offered in sacrifice, and to offer everything in sacrifice, as the Gita says, is to follow the example of God Himself.

Krishna, who is speaking in the name of the personal God, says, "I have no work to do in all the worlds, Arjuna, for all these worlds are mine. I have nothing to obtain because I have all, yet I work." The whole work of creation is not necessary to God, but God has created this world and God works in this world. "If I was not bound to action, never tiring everlastingly, men who follow many paths would follow my path of inaction. But if ever my work had an end these worlds would end in destruction. Confusion would reign within all, this would be the death of all beings." The whole world is sustained by the action of God. We have to unite our action with the action of God, and then our action has a divine character. Sacrifice is to make a thing sacred, to make it over to God so that it becomes something divine.

So we offer everything we do to God, and in doing so we

are copying the action of God. Jesus himself said, "My Father worketh hitherto, and I work." "The Son does nothing but what he sees the Father doing." Every work has to be done in the light of God. God is working in you. You are carrying out His action.

Krishna now sums it up, "Offer to me all thy works and rest thy mind on the Supreme. Be free from vain hopes and selfish thoughts." It is these vain hopes, ambitions, desires and selfish thoughts which are the cause of trouble. We are occupied with ourselves and so become disturbed and anxious. But the Gita counsels us, "With inner peace, fight thou the fight." Go on, do the work however difficult it may be, but with the inner peace which comes from the fact that you have surrendered yourself to God. You can see what a deep teaching this is. Mahatma Gandhi fought the British by these rules of the Bhagavad-Gita, and he won the battle.

Now we come to a still deeper level. We try to do our work without seeking a reward, we leave the results to God; we offer our work in sacrifice, uniting ourselves with the action of God. Our action becomes a kind of Eucharist. It is God who is acting in us. This is beautifully expressed in the fourth book of the Bhagavad-Gita: "Who, in all his work sees God, he in truth goes to God. God is his worship, God is his offering, offered by God in the fire of God."

I must mention that Mascaro's translation is aimed at western readers. When he uses the word God, as he does here, I think it is perfectly excusable, but the word is *Brahman*. And Brahman is neuter. It is not precisely the same as God. It is difficult to try to translate these words. I think we can in fact translate Brahman, that is, *Nirguna Brahman*, 'Brahman without attributes,' as the Godhead. That is probably the best translation. Then *Saguna Brahman*, 'God with attributes,' is the personal God. So Brahman can be used both of the Godhead and of the personal God.

So it reads: "Who in all his work, sees Brahman, he in truth goes to Brahman; Brahman is his worship, Brahman is his offering, offered by Brahman in the fire of Brahman." Now that really is a Eucharistic action. In the Eucharist God is worshipped. You offer what you are doing to God. At the same time it is God Himself who makes the offering and who is being offered. God is both priest and victim. And it is offered in the fire of God: the action itself is a sacrifice and the fire is the fire of God's love in which the sacrifice is offered.

So every action should be a Eucharistic action, that is the goal, to be united with Christ in His offering, so that one's total life is offered to God. The offering is God Himself, He is offering Himself in us, in the fire of His own love, that is by the power of His own grace, resulting in a totally transformed human life. That is to make one's whole life a sacrifice. That is the goal of offering work.

Another way of putting it is to say, "Work should be no work." It is very difficult to translate this phrase. One could perhaps translate it best by "action in inaction." There is a beautiful Chinese equivalent in the expression *Wuwei*. Wuwei in Chinese means active passivity, or passive activity. We need to learn this more than anything else — how to be active and yet passive at the same time. In other words, while there is something in us which acts — my hands, my voice, my mind, my will, all my faculties are acting, fully engaged — there should at the same time be a centre of peace, of repose, of quiet, behind all the activity. The activity takes place in the midst of inaction.

I often use the illustration of the fingers and the palm of the hand. The fingers represent the faculties, the senses, the feelings, the imagination, the mind, the reason and the will. We use all our faculties in our work, whatever we are doing. But just as the fingers spring from the palm of the hand, the faculties spring from the centre of the soul. Every action of the senses, of the feelings, the imagination, of the mind and the will should spring from the centre of inner peace where we are united with God. If it is offered in this way the action is effective; it is skill in action. But if not, then the action is ineffective. We get tired because we allow ourselves to be carried away by our activities, and then our faculties also tire. But they should always be being renewed in their centre.

We take time for prayer and meditation and retreat and recollection in order to renew all our faculties, to get back into ourselves. Then we can go out refreshed. That is the basic aim of transcendental meditation. Maharishi Mahesh Yogi maintains that if you meditate properly for twenty minutes in the morning and twenty minutes in the evening you can renew all your faculties. You can get down to a deep centre of rest and then, from that centre of rest, you can be more effective and more efficient in your work. Everybody today, in the church and outside of it, is involved in the great problem of action which absorbs us continually, at every level. The question is how to act from the inner centre of peace: how to find that centre and then to act from it.

This is action which comes from inaction; or an active inactivity as we may call it; or we can call it contemplation in action. In recent times there has been a disastrous division between contemplation and action. Some people are contemplative, some active. That is a false division. Some people are more contemplative, no doubt; some people are more active. But surely what we want in the Church and in the world is a contemplation which unites us with God at a vertical level where we transcend ourselves, the world and all our problems, and experience oneness with God; and at the same time, a mode of action at the horizontal level by which we go out from the centre of peace in God to the whole world. The further we go vertically towards God, the further we can go horizontally towards man.

Jesus is the man who is totally given to God, to the Father, the one who is totally surrendered to the vertical movement, so that the Son always sees what the Father is doing. At the same time he was totally open to all creation, to all people, and to life as a whole. That is the dual movement, vertical and horizontal, of contemplation and action, action in contemplation. That is the universal call not only for monks or for nuns or for unmarried people, but for everybody who seeks to live a Christian life or who seeks God.

So we have not to seek the fruit of the work but to offer our work in sacrifice, in a spirit of devotion, of *bhakti*, that is, of love, to God. Finally, we have to reach the stage when we can say, "I am not the doer." That is the climax.

" 'I am not doing the work,' thinks the man who is in harmony, who sees the truth. For in seeing, or in hearing, or in smelling, or in touching, or eating, or walking, or sleeping, or breathing, in talking, or grasping, or relaxing, or even in opening or closing his eyes, he remembers, 'It is the servants of my soul that are working.' "

"I am not the doer." The Spirit of God is working in me and he is using my mind, my body, my faculties, everything that I am. I am the instrument. This is what St Paul meant when he said, "I live, yet I no longer, it is Christ who lives in me."

Ramakrishna, the Hindu saint of the last century, always emphasized this point. "I am not the doer." If you say "I am the doer," then your ego gets in. "I have done this, or I am going to do that." It is not you. You have surrendered yourself. There is another beautiful saying from St Paul: "You are dead and your life is hidden with Christ in God." Your ego is dead. That is crucifixion; and everything you do comes from this inner centre of your being where Christ dwells in your heart.

This leads to a further stage. It is found in the Upanishads but is given a further meaning in the Bhagavad-Gita. "Such a man sees himself in the heart of all beings, and all beings in his heart. This is the vision of the Yogi of harmony, a vision which is ever one."

When you have learned to see yourself in all beings, in all creation, in the earth, the trees, and the flowers, the birds and animals, in the streets and shops, and in every person, then you discover the Lord dancing in the world and in every human heart. The yogi sees all beings in himself and himself in the heart of all beings.

Now the Bhagavad-Gita takes it a step further and says, "He sees me in all and all in me, and then I never leave Him and He never leaves me." In other words this Brahman, this Atman in the heart of creation is a personal God. You see that person in yourself and you see yourself in Him, and then, it says, "I never leave Him and He never leaves me." We have reached the centre of personal communion with God. This is the goal of karma yoga.

So that is the first part of the Gita, that of karma yoga. The next stage is bhakti yoga, the worship of a personal God. Here I want to make a few points to add to those which I made previously about the personal God. The question in Hinduism is always how far this God, this personal God, transcends the creation. He always tends to be involved in the creation. Is He really transcendent?

This is a serious issue, I believe, between the Hindu and the Christian. The Hindu tends to allow God to blend with the world. The Christian wants a total transcendence. Here in the Bhagavad-Gita we have the clearest expression, in all the Hindu Scriptures that I know, of this total transcendence. This is very important. At this point, at least, the Hindu mind rose to the sense that God is totally above creation. Here Krishna says, "The visible forms of my nature are eight. Earth, water, fire, air, ether, the mind, reason, and a sense of

'I.' '' That is the whole creation. The five elements in the
Hindu tradition which make up the world of the senses and
the three functions of the human mind are a form of God.
This sounds pantheistic, but later it is corrected. When people say this is pantheism they do not realize that Hindus are
using language in a particular way.

Manikka Vasakar, the great Tamil poet, once said, "You
are all that exists and You are nothing that exists." He is in
everything and yet He is beyond everything. This is made
clear in the present text.

Krishna says, "The visible forms of my nature are these,
but beyond my visible nature is my invisible spirit. This is the
fountain of life whereby this universe has its being. All things
have their life in this life, but I am their beginning and end."
So He is above and beyond all. In the next book he makes it
slightly more explicit. He goes a step further:

Krishna says, "Beyond this creation, both visible and invisible, there is a higher invisible Eternal, and when all things
pass away, this remains forever."

This creation, the material world, is visible; the mind, the
consciousness, is invisible. But beyond the material, visible
world, beyond the psychological world, the world of the
mind, of human consciousness, there is this other invisible
unmanifest.

"This invisible is called the Everlasting, and is the end, Supreme. Those who reach Him never return. This is my Supreme Abode. This Supreme Person, Arjuna, is attained by
an ever living love."

This Supreme Person called *Purushottoman* is above both
the visible and the invisible. He is the Supreme Lord of all.
This is clear enough but becomes clearer still in the next
book, where Krishna says, "All this universe comes from my
invisible Being. All beings have their rest in me, but I have
not my rest in them." What he means is, "All things depend

on me, but I do not depend on them." And that, of course, is exactly the Christian doctrine. God creates the world, the world totally depends on God, but God does not depend in any way on the world. Then he goes even further. In case it may still mistakenly be thought that there is some dependence he says, "And, in truth, they rest not in me. Consider my sacred mystery. I am the source of all beings, I support them all, but I rest not in them." Saying he rests in them may still suggest that he depends on them, so he adds, "I am their source, I support them but I rest not in them."

This "sacred mystery" is Mascaro's translation of the word *maya*. One must be very careful about the word *maya*. It can and later does mean 'illusion,' the illusion of the world, but in the original sense it was something much deeper. It is sometimes translated, "my magic power," and originally it was the creative power. Maya was God's power in creation. God was the *mayin*, the 'maker,' and maya was the power that made the world.

Then we have an interesting distinction in Chapter Fifteen. He again distinguishes three elements. These words, *Brahman, Atman* and *Purusha* are, as I said, words which signify the Supreme Reality, but they can be used at different levels. Brahman can be *nirguna Brahman*, absolute transcendence, beyond all comprehension. He can be *saguna Brahman*, Brahman with attributes, the Lord, the Creator. And further — this is confusing to us — he can be the visible universe in which he manifests himself, so that sometimes this world is said to be Brahman. This is a real difficulty: words in Indian thought are fluid in this way. We want them categorized to know exactly what they mean. But the words can move from one sphere to another, and only by the context can one see the real difference between them.

So also with *Atman*: there is the *Paramatman*, the 'Supreme Being;' the Atman in man which is the Spirit of God in man; but *Atman* can also be the 'spirit of man.'

The same is true of *Purusha*. The 'Supreme Person,' *Purushottoman*, is the Supreme above all, and he manifests in the human person. Each one of us is a purusha. Even this body as the expression of the person can be called a purusha. It is confusing, I admit, but it is important to see how the words can be used at different levels.

"There are two purushas or spirits in this universe: the perishable and the imperishable. The perishable is all things in creation, the imperishable is that which moves not." That is to say, the imperishable is consciousness, the mind. So you have the material purusha and the immaterial. But the highest spirit, the highest Purusha, is another. It is called the Purushottoman, the Supreme Spirit, the Supreme Person. He is the God of eternity who pervades all, sustains all. "Because I am beyond the perishable and even beyond the imperishable, in this world and in the Vedas I am known as Purushottoman, the Spirit Supreme. He who with a clear vision sees me as a Supreme Person, he knows all there is to be known and he adores me with all his soul. I have revealed to thee the most secret doctrine, Arjuna. He who sees it sees light and his task in this world is done." So that is the revelation of the Supreme in the Bhagavad-Gita.

The Gita comes to a climax in the famous Tenth and Eleventh Chapters, with the great theophany in which the whole creation appears in the body of Krishna. It is very poetic, very magnificent, but it does not add anything to what we have been discussing.

Let us go on to the last six books. We have seen *karma-marga*, the 'way of work,' and *bhaktimarga*, the 'way of devotion' to the Lord. Now we will look at *jnanamarga*, the 'way of knowledge.'

These ways can be separated, but Hindus today tend to see

them as three paths which converge. Most people today are karma yogis. Nearly all Christians are karma yogis; they see the way to God through work, through service. This is a perfectly valid way, of course, but if we simply remain on the level of karma alone we will not fulfill our goal.

I have heard tragic stories of people of very good will who go out into the slums to do work for God. I knew of one group in Brazil, priests and sisters, and others, who went to work in the slums, and their idea was that you found Christ in your neighbour. You did not need a church, you did not need to pray. I do not believe the priests even said Mass. They just worked for God.

Well, it was a beautiful idea in its way, but a friend who was with them told me that at the end of six years the whole thing totally collapsed. Karma yoga, without the support of bhakti and jnana, is not adequate. We have all got to find a way to sustain our work. And that is where bhakti yoga comes in, the yoga of love, and jnana yoga, the yoga of knowledge.

In the Christian tradition contemplation is really knowledge of love, knowledge by love. Love has to go into our work, and love has to go into our knowledge.

There is a passage in the letter to the Ephesians which brings this out exactly: "You may know the love of Christ which passes knowledge." It is knowledge of love. St Paul says elsewhere, "The love of God is poured into our hearts by the Holy Spirit who is given us." Many people do not know that love. It is given them in baptism, it is sealed in confirmation, it may be renewed in the Eucharist; but to know that love is to reflect on it, to realise it, to experience it in the heart. This is the nature of religious experience: it is a knowledge of love. But it is also a love that passes knowledge. It is not a rational love, not a thinking about love or a thinking about Christ; it is experiencing that love in the heart. It is an intuitive understanding.

The traditional definition of contemplation is that it is knowledge by love. That is Christian contemplation. So bhakti enters into our work and bhakti, love, enters into our knowledge. In this way we grow to this knowledge of love.

In the Middle Ages they disputed the question of whether the beatific vision consists primarily of knowledge or primarily of love. St Bonaventure said it was love and St Thomas said it was knowledge. This can still be debated. But what actually happens is that as we converge on this ultimate, all the faculties and powers of our being converge in unity and we experience God in the totality of our being. Ultimately, in the Resurrection the totality of body and soul experience the mystery of God. There is a total transformation of body and soul in this love-knowledge.

The Bhagavad-Gita concludes in the eighteenth chapter with these wonderful words: "Hear again my Word Supreme, the deepest secret of silence. Because I love thee well, I will speak to thee words of salvation."

This is one of the supreme moments in history, when it dawned upon man that God loves him. Bhakti is man's love for God and there has always been bhakti, devotion to God. But that God loves man, that is something more, and that is what Krishna says: "Because I love thee well, I will speak to thee words of salvation."

"Give thy mind to me, give me thy heart and thy sacrifice and thy adoration. This is my word of promise, thou shalt in truth come to me for thou art dear to me." The word is *priya*, 'dear to me.' "Leave all things behind and come to me for salvation. I will make thee free from the bondage of sin, fear no more."

This is India's gospel of salvation and love. I once went to a meeting at a seminary in India run by the Jesuits. The rector, who was very enterprising, organised a seminar on salvation. He invited a Muslim and two Hindus to give talks on salvation in Islam, salvation in Vaishnavism, and salvation in Shaivism.

The two Hindus were most interesting. They were both very learned *pandits*, or 'leaders,' of their sect. Both said that for them God was a God of love. It was through His grace that man was drawn to Him, and the end of life was union in love with God.

That is the essential teaching of the gospel, is it not? But let us remember that all this is said in a different context, and we use these words in a slightly, subtly different sense. In the next talk we will look at the ideas *avatara* and "incarnation," to see what the difference is between Christian revelation and this cosmic revelation.

God reveals Himself in creation and reveals Himself in the heart of man. By entering into his heart man discovers not only that he can love God, but that he is loved by God. There is no doubt about it. When one reads the bhakti poets of India their love for God is astounding, and their sense of God's love for them is overwhelming.

In the next talk I would like to try to draw out the distinctive characteristics of the Biblical revelation, and see how it can be related to this. But we should never forget or deny that God reveals Himself in the most wonderful way to those who seek Him. The Bhagavad-Gita is a treasure of God's revelation of His love to man.

Christian Revelation

I want to try to relate the Cosmic Revelation as we have seen it — especially in Hinduism — to the Christian Revelation. Whether, or how, this can be done is a fundamental question for us all. It is not an easy question to answer.

For a long time Christians have been willing to dismiss other religions as false religions. It has been said that Christianity is the one true religion, and Christians have not felt disturbed in any way. But when we begin to discover the truth in other religions, when we enter deeply into them, we realise how much God has given to them. Then the problems arise.

The Cosmic Revelation is based on the belief that God reveals Himself in creation and in the human soul. In Hinduism, in particular, we have seen how the Cosmic Revelation has led not merely to a depth of understanding and knowledge, but to a real love of God. When we consider how the Cosmic Revelation extends throughout the world we recognize what values there are in this universal revelation, many of which we ourselves have lost.

As regards Hinduism, we saw that it speaks of the Cosmic Mystery as revealed in the world, under the name of Brahman. The Cosmic Mystery itself is beyond words, beyond thought. It is an inexpressible mystery, manifesting itself in the cosmos; infinitely transcendent and not to be uttered;

neti, neti: 'not this, not this.' It manifests in the whole creation, so that the whole creation is filled with the presence of God. Creation, in other words, is sacramental. That surely is something that we all need to discover — the presence of God in this world around us.

We saw how Hinduism conceives of this Cosmic Mystery, present in man as the Atman, the Spirit in man. Once again it is both transcendent and immanent. Paramatman, the Supreme Spirit, is beyond word and thought, yet it is present in man in the depths of his spirit. So the spirit of man meets the Spirit of God and we experience His presence.

I have emphasised all along how this is not a theory or a doctrine, but an experience. When we enter into the depths of our soul, or rather the depths of our own spirit, we discover this depth of God, the Lord dwelling within us. That is the third aspect: this Brahman, this Atman, is the Lord, is a Person, a cosmic Person, who dwells in the heart of every creature, and of every human being, yet embraces the whole creation and is beyond all humanity. He is the *Purushottoman*, the 'Supreme Person' beyond and above all.

We can hardly deny that the Cosmic Revelation has shown the Hindu the real transcendence and the immanence of God in creation and in man. We saw in the Bhagavad-Gita how this Cosmic Lord is not only a Lord to be worshipped and adored, but also that he loves his worshipper; "Give me thy heart," he says, "give me thy sacrifice, give me thy adoration." But he is also a Lord who has love for man: "You are dear to me." This is a real revelation of divine love.

I cannot help thinking that it is significant that this Revelation appears in the Vedas, Upanishads, and the Bhagavad-Gita in the centuries before the time of Christ. Karl Jaspers has called this period the "axial period in human history." In the first milennium B.C. there seems to have taken place a universal awakening to the transcendent mystery. It flowered in the tradition of the Vedas with the Upanishads, in the sixth century, B.C. It was renewed by the Buddha at almost the same time with the experience of Nirvana, that state beyond the world of becoming. It was discovered by Confucius and Lao Tsu in China about the same time. The Tao of Lao Tsu is one of the most profound expressions of this cosmic mystery. "The Tao that can be named," it says, "is not the eternal Tao." There is a Tao, a Way, which is beyond the order of this world. There is an eternal order which cannot be named; when it is named, it is "the mother of all things."

This awakening occured in Persia at about the same time. Zoroaster had a conception of the Supreme Good opposed to the power of evil. It was found in the Greek philosophers in Heraclitus in the sixth century, and in Socrates, of whom Justin Martyr said that the Logos which had been revealed to the Jews was known also to Socrates and Heraclitus among the Greeks.

At this very time, the sixth century B.C., the divine mystery revealed itself to the Hebrew Prophets Isaiah, Jeremiah and Ezekiel. Here is surely a convergence, and it makes us feel that human history is one. When Christians think of sacred history they sometimes confine it to Biblical history; but surely there is a sacred history which embraces the world. The primitive tribes of America, as well as those of Africa and of Australia, all have known something of this revelation which goes back tens of thousands of years.

In the first milennium B.C. this great movement seems to have come to a head; a breakthrough took place in all these different spheres, and practically all the deepest principles of religion in the world today derive from the great revelations which took place during that time.

As we come nearer to the time of Christ we find in the Bhagavad-Gita and the Svetasvatara Upanishad a deeper understanding, a sense of the person of God, and finally of the love of God. Surely this is a divine dispensation.

One can speak as De Smet has done of a "holy history" of India, from the Vedas, through the Upanishads and the Bhagavad-Gita, and then to the great bhakti poets, the poets of devotion, who went around to the different temples singing hymns of love and adoration for a particular form of God, but really going through that form to God Himself.

Later, there was a Muslim influence in India. One of the greatest examples was Kabir, a mystical poet. Nobody knows whether he was Hindu or Muslim. There is a story that at his death when he was laid out for the last rites the Hindus claimed him for cremation and the Muslims for burial, but when they went to take the body all they found was a heap of flowers — this was a wonderful moment when the two religious traditions met in one man.

Then there has been a Christian influence upon Hinduism in modern times. From the 19th Century onwards there have been many educated Hindus who have been deeply influenced by the New Testament. So this "holy history" goes on.

In the Bhagavad-Gita we come to a crucial point where the revelation is made that God loves man — not only that man loves God, but God loves man. In this love between God and man, we find the principle of grace. God is love, and He communicates His love by grace. He delivers man from sin and unites him with Himself by His grace. Here we come to something very close to the gospel. Christians so easily dismiss Hinduism as pantheism, monism or polytheism without realising that, although those elements are present, God, the word of God, is revealing Himself to them, and the Spirit of God is present to them.

So much of the gospel appears to be already there. The question arises for the Christian, what is the point of preaching the gospel? What have we got to say to the Hindu? This is made more difficult by the fact that the Hindu is perfectly convinced that he has the whole truth. This is something one has to face and one does face day by day. Our founder, Father Monchanin, came to India with a wonderful vision of an Indian Church, hoping for dialogue with Hindus. He was terribly frustrated because he found no curiosity among them. They feel they have the absolute and final truth. Vedanta is the final word of truth.

All religions are, for them, included in this one truth. We have a neighbour in India, the head of an excellent ashram, a great pandit who goes around the country giving lectures and retreats. He has the absolute conviction that Vedanta is the one Supreme Truth and that all religions, including Christianity, are included in Vedanta. For them there is nothing to be learned. Christianity is simply one form of *sanatanadharma*, this 'Eternal Religion,' which developed in the West and is adapted to Western mentality. Islam is another form which developed in the Middle East, in Arabia, and is adapted to those people. They always say that each person can have his own religion; it can be any religion you like, but all religion is ultimately the same and all end in the same identity of Being. For them there is no problem, there is no conflict, but there is also no dialogue. That is our problem, how to differentiate between the different religions. In all my experience in India in twenty-five years, I have hardly ever found an educated Hindu who is really open to dialogue, who really wanted to understand Christian faith as something "other."

Once we had a wonderful meeting at Ootacamund, a station in the Nilgiri Hills in South India. It was organised by some members of the Society of Friends. We had a mixed group of Christians of different churches, and of Hindus, about thirty in all. We shared together for ten days. There were professors there from Benares Hindu University, who had had Christian students among their pupils — one of them had a Christian student who was studying St John's Gospel

— and in them I found a certain curiosity, a certain awakening, a feeling that here was something that had a new meaning for them. But this is very rare indeed.

There is no doubt that God has revealed Himself in a wonderful way in India for all these thousands of years: He has revealed Himself in creation; He has revealed Himself in the human heart; and above all perhaps, He has revealed Himself in a succession of Saints.

Nothing moves the Hindu more than the attraction of these holy men who, from the time of the Vedas through the Buddha, from Rama and Krishna and the *bhaktas*, the 'devotees,' with their mystical poetry, to Shankara and Ramanuja, the great doctors of Vedanta, are a continuing source of inspiration right up to the present day. Every Hindu has his own particular saint whom he venerates as his guru and many others for whom he has a special devotion.

In modern times Gandhi was known to everybody as the *Mahatma*, the 'great soul.' Rabindrath Tagore was called Guru Dev, the divine guru. Sri Aurobindo was called Mahayogi, the great yogi. I personally consider him the greatest philosopher of modern India, with the deepest insight into the ultimate nature of reality. For many years I studied him and I have never forgotten my debt to him. In addition there is Ramana Maharshi, the 'great rishi,' considered the most holy man of modern India, a man of great purity of heart who had the deepest experience of the Atman, the inner Spirit, and the greatest compassion for others.

This succession of saints presents a challenge to the Christian Church and to western society. At present this challenge is only beginning to be realised. We are bound to face this challenge in all its dimensions, just as the Christian Fathers faced the challenge of Plato and Aristotle and Greek philosophy as a whole.

Let us seek to discern what the specific character of Hinduism is, and try to do it objectively. First of all there is its mythological character: Hinduism is rooted first in the mythology of the Vedas, and then that of the Epics and Puranas. The whole religion is based on mythology, and every temple is built around some mythological story. We no longer despise mythology today. A myth is a symbolic story which expresses, in symbolic terms which rise from the depths of the unconscious, man's understanding of God and the mystery of existence. Myths are of infinite value and importance. I do not think it is too strong to say that God revealed Himself from the earliest times in the form of myth. Let me say, therefore, that to say that Hinduism is rooted in mythology is not to depreciate it in any way. Every religion is derived from a mythology, and the Hindu religion is particularly rich in mythology. However, we have to admit that since mythology arises from the archetypal images of the Unconscious it lives in the world of the imagination, and it is always in danger of fantasy. To bring the myth into relation with historic reality is always a problem.

In Hinduism there are great philosophers who reflect on the myths and bring out their deep significance. And there are mystics who make the myth a means of communion with the Supreme God. Mythology sustains Hinduism right up to the present day. But it has some very obvious dangers. There is always the element of fantasy, and always an element of ambivalence. The myth is always fluid and its hold on reality is uncertain. I have always found it baffling when talking even to educated Hindus to see how easily their minds move from what we would call a sphere of history and philosophy to a sphere of myth and fantasy. They will speak of some person of today — Ramakrishna, or Mahatma Gandhi — and the next moment they will speak of Krishna and his sporting with the Gopis, as though they were on exactly the same level. They seem to move from the historic and the philosophical to the imaginative plane without any demarcation. In the West we want clearer demarcations. This has certain advantages, but we have to recognise that it also has limitations. It can help to clarify concepts, but often leads to real dichotomy in life.

This is also found in India today. I have an English scientist friend who spent four years in an international scientific institute in India. He said that almost all his Indian colleagues kept their science on one side and their religion on another. As scientists they simply accepted a materialistic or atheistic view of things. They were not concerned with religion in any way, but at home they would go on with their mythology, their worship of the gods without any apparent relationship between the two.

This means that many Hindus ultimately give up their religion. They often leave it to their wives. They themselves become practically agnostic, and this is leading to a real crisis in India. In the universities the typical lecturer, professor, or educated student begins to lose his faith. A great testing is going to come about as a result of this problem of mythology.

We must not despise the myth. Myths have given us wonderful insights into the mystery of the cosmos and into the mystery of the human soul. But the myth needs to be corrected by reason and by science, where science means a knowledge of the concrete reality of things. It has to be freed from this ambivalence, and above all from all moral ambivalence. There are great problems. It is very much what Plato found with the Homeric myths. Plato banished Homer and the poets from his ideal Republic because he said they told stories about the gods which were quite inappropriate.

So also the stories of Krishna, or almost any of the gods of Hinduism, are full of immoral incidents. They can be given, it is true, an allegorical interpretation. For instance, take the story of Krishna and the Gopis: Krishna is the charming cowherd who plays on his flute and all the Gopis, the women cowherds, come and flock to him, to dance with him in the moonlight. They leave their husbands and their families to dance with him. This was taken allegorically to be the love of God drawing people from family and everything to surrender themselves to Him alone. There is also the story of how Krishna found the Gopis bathing one day and he stole their clothes and hid them up in a tree. Then he made them all come out of the water naked. They were terribly ashamed and he only gave them back their clothes when they had all come back to him. There again, this signifies allegorically that when you come to God you are stripped of all your ego, of all externals; you must be naked before God.

These are beautiful allegorical stories but you can see that the ordinary person can interpret them in many other ways, and they have been interpreted in ways that have led to extreme eroticism in the worship of Krishna.

Krishna is said, like Solomon, to have had forty thousand wives and concubines. Again one can find an allegorical interpretation of it, but it belongs to a whole world of mythology and of moral ambivalence. An educated Hindu, a philosophical Hindu, will explain them very much as the Greek philosophers in the time of St Augustine explained the Greek and Roman myths, but the moral ambivalence remains, and its effect on the people is considerable. It has led to gross immorality at times, and always to a certain ambiguity.

Then we come to the question of a lack of historical perspective. There is very little history in ancient India. The epics and the puranas are all mythological history. There is some evidence that there was a great war, which was recorded in the Mahabharata like the Trojan war recorded by Homer, but it has been almost completely transported into the realm of mythology. The Indian people as a whole did not seem to develop a sense of historical reality. As a result the world was seen more and more as *samsara*, as a place of continual recurrence — "The Myth of the Eternal Return," as Mircea Eliade has called it. Everything comes into being and then passes away. This applies even to the creation of the world. The whole world comes forth from Brahma, and it goes through all its stages of evolution. We are living in what is called the *kali yuga*, the worst stage of all, when everything is going into corruption. Then a new cycle will begin and everything will come into being again.

The whole sense of time in the Hindu and Oriental perspective is cyclic. They live in a world of cyclic time because it is a world based on the cosmic order: When we look around the world we see that everything moves in cycles. The sun rises and sets, the moon waxes and wanes, spring is followed by summer, autumn, and winter, to be followed by spring again.

Out of this arises the doctrine of karma. You are born, you grow up, you die, and you are born again; this is the wheel of samsara. The great struggle of the Hindu saint, and in a sense the great aim of Hindu philosophy, was to escape from this wheel of time: to get free from this world of time, space, and matter, and to experience that ultimate reality, that ultimate oneness of being which is beyond time and space and matter and limitation.

It is a wonderful search, but it leaves out the reality of this world. I cannot help feeling that the present situation of India, with its masses of poor, illiterate people, of people suffering from disease and being left to die in the streets, really stems from this basic philosophy — all are caught in this wheel of samsara. Your karma has brought you to this state where you are dying in the street, but when you have died you will be reborn, and, please God, you will have a better birth next time. If one can help somebody else to have a better birth, if one can help him on his way, that is good; but there is no obligation to do it. Karma is working itself out.

This sense of cyclic time and constant recurrence can, of course, lead to a terrible fatalism, which can be sad but which can also be very sustaining. The Hindu peasant, the poor man, has a wonderful capacity to endure because he simply says, "All these things come from God" — disease, suffering, death, your child dies, your wife dies, all this is part of karma, part of the cosmic order.

But there is no sense of progress, no sense that you can get beyond these things, except in going beyond altogether to realise Brahman. That can be done through the grace of God. You pray to God and He will set you free from the wheel of time.

We have to see Hindu doctrine and Hindu sanctity within the context of karma, samsara, and the whole mythological world of the Vedas and the Epics and the Puranas. The modern Hindu is trying to escape the negative aspect of myth, to realise more of the value of history, of matter, of science, and of progress. Dr. Radhakrishnan, for instance, a leading scholar among Hindus, has been much influenced by the West and tries to bring out these aspects. But the opposite tendency remains very strong. That, I think, is the negative aspect of Hinduism.

Now let us compare that with the Hebrew revelation. It seems to me that what the Hebrew brought into human experience was this movement from myth to history. The story of the creation in Genesis and of Adam and Eve in Paradise are myths in the proper sense. They are symbolic stories revealing the mystery of the creation of man, of his relation to God, how he has fallen from his communion with God, how he is exposed to the forces of this world, and so on. These are wonderful myths, symbolic stories.

In the following chapters of Genesis, beginning with Noah and the Ark, we pass from myth to legend. Myth, that is cosmic myth, is based on imaginative insight into the rhythm of the cosmos, the universe, whereas legend begins from historic persons and situations and then, from that historic event, builds up a symbolic understanding, a mystical understanding, of the meaning of that person's life for humanity and for the world. Noah is obviously a legendary character, and the flood and the survival of that one family is a symbol of the periodic destruction and re-creation of the world.

According to recent biblical scholarship, (particularly that of Roland De Vaux, a Dominican who spent his life at the Biblical School in Jerusalem), it seems that the stories of Abraham, Isaac, and Jacob are legends which have come together from different sources and have been developed into a kind of myth, the story of God's dealings with mankind.

In Moses we come closer to the light of history, but again, there is a mythological background to the whole story of the Exodus and the journey through the desert. Ancient man was much more interested in the symbolic meaning of things; how they showed God's action in history, rather than in particular historical facts.

But the Hebrew was coming more and more to understand that God acts in history. The fundamental difference between the Hebrew and the Hindu Revelation is that the latter is the revelation of God's work in creation, and the former is the revelation of God's work in history, the history of a particular people. God intervened in the history of that people, first of all in the lives of Abraham, Isaac, and Jacob, out of a more or less legendary background; then in the life of Moses, where we come into the light of history, (though legend is still built up around it), and then through Joshua, until we come to Samuel, David, and Solomon. With the books of Samuel we are in the clear light of history. They were apparently written almost contemporaneously, and anybody who reads them knows they are full of the sordid details of human life as it really is.

Hebrew understanding emerged from the mythological background. The Hebrew name for God, *Elohim*, was plural. It signified the world of the 'gods,' of the divine Mystery. Then it was realised that this divine mystery was revealed in the person of Yahweh, who had revealed Himself to Moses on Mount Sinai. Gradually this mythic background was focused in history. God, Yahweh, leads his people through historic time towards an end. There is no longer any sense of cyclic time. God leads His people towards an end, when He will finally reveal Himself. He makes a promise to Abraham, "Go out from your country to the land which I will show you and I will make you a great people." This is a revelation of God's action in history in the actual world of the Middle East.

When we come to the great prophets — Amos, and Hosea, Isaiah, Jeremiah and Ezekiel — we are right at the centre of history. The prophets are concerned with the history of their people, of God's action in Israel's concrete situation, and the actual demands which God makes.

This brought a historic dimension into human understanding. Of course with Herodotus the Greeks also began to write history at this time, but they did not link their history with their religion. Their religion remained mythological, their history secular. But Israel understood the myth, the *Mythos*, the revelation of the divine, the cosmic mystery, in the light of historic events and the history of their own people.

So when we come to the Prophets we find God revealing Himself in a historic situation, and here the moral amivalence begins to disappear. In the early part of the Bible there is still a good deal of ambivalence. It cannot be said that Yahweh is a fully moral being at many stages. Even in the Psalms there are times when He is simply the God of Israel, the God of hosts who helps destroy Israel's enemies, reminding us of the God who in the Book of Samuel commands them to destroy a town with all the men, women, and children in it. There is a moral ambivalence still in Yahweh, but as the Prophets come nearer to God, to a deeper understanding, gradually that moral ambivalence is removed and He is seen to be a God of absolute holiness and justice.

I do not think that one can find anywhere in Hinduism and Buddhism a comparable conception of the holiness of God which is essentially a moral holiness. It is a holiness which demands holiness in His people: "Be you holy because I the Lord your God am holy," it is said in Leviticus, and holiness involves justice to your neighbour. Isaiah said, "To what purpose are your sacrifices and your vain oblations? Learn to do well, seek judgement, relieve the oppressed, judge the fatherless, plead for the widow." This is a tremendous movement away from a mythological understanding of the world towards a historic understanding. God is acting in the history of His people, and when they reject the orphan and the widow and the poor they reject God. This is something new.

Israel discovered the moral aspect of God and removed the ambivalence. Yet one may feel that the conception of God of the Old Testament is still somewhat narrow in regard to His justice and even to His holiness, and we have to wait till the New Testament for the final Revelation, when all ambivalence is removed.

This conception of history leads to a completely different conception of time. Time is no longer cyclic; time is moving towards an end, an *eschaton*. That is something completely new, and something unique in Israel. The God of Israel is acting in history and is leading mankind towards an end, an eschaton, a final stage.

That breaks through the whole idea of samsara, the wheel of time. Time is not something from which man has to escape but time is something which is leading him towards an end. This makes a profound difference in one's understanding of life. Our actual human life, our deeds from day to day belong to an eternal order, and reveal the direction in which the world is moving. All things are under the providence of God and are leading to a final fulfillment. With the coming of Christ we encounter this finality.

Here we come to the great difference between an *avatara* and an incarnation. Most Hindus translate the word *avatara* as 'incarnation.' It means literally a 'descent,' a descent of God. The concept of avatara is given clear expression for the first time in the Bhagavad-Gita, where Krishna says to Arjuna, "When *dharma* [righteousness] declines, and *adharma* [unrighteousness] prevails, then I take birth." So an avatara is a descent of God to restore the order of righteousness. The Hindu speaks of that as an incarnation.

When we compare the Avatara with the Incarnation we can see that the Avatara has its roots in mythology. There are usually said to be ten avataras. The first was a fish, the second was a tortoise, the third a boar, the fourth a man-lion, the fifth a dwarf, the sixth was a hero, and the seventh and eighth were Rama and Krishna, who are the supreme avataras.

The modern Hindu interprets this to mean that at every stage of evolution, God has intervened in the history of the world. When water covered the earth God took the form of a fish; when the earth was coming from under the water He took the form of a tortoise; and when the animals were ranging freely He took the form of a boar. When the animals were beginning to evolve to man He took the form of a man-lion, Narasimha. When man had emerged in a very primitive form He took the form of a dwarf. When man had gone further, to the heroic age, He took the form of the hero, Parasurama; and finally, when man had reached his full evolution, He took a human form, as Rama and Krishna. Rama is the Lord of Righteousness. The whole aim of Rama is to restore the dharma. Krishna is the God of Love. He and Rama together

represent righteousness and love. Modern Hindus see the avatara as revealing God at every stage of creation and coming to
a head in Rama and Krishna.

But again, both Rama and Krishna are heroes of epic
poems. We know practically nothing of them outside the
Ramayana and the Mahabharata and the still more mythological stories of the Puranas. There is a reference to Krishna,
son of Devaki, in the Upanishads, but that is all. They are
legendary figures, originally historical, like Hector or
Achilles in Homer, but clearly legendary and living in a world
of mythology.

There are beautiful stories about Krishna when he was a
baby which led to the worship of the Child Krishna, the *Bala
Krishna*. One day he stole the butter, and when he was eating
it his mother got annoyed with him. Then he opened his
mouth, and in his mouth she saw the whole creation. So the
little child was really God. It is all a world of myth, and
deeply significant, but not fully historical.

The modern Hindu would add further incarnations. In a
typical Hindu gesture Buddha was taken into this pantheon
and was made a ninth avatara. Finally, at the end of time
there is to be the Kalki avatara. He is to come at the end of
the world and bring everything to a conclusion. The modern
Hindu also includes holy men of the present day. They will
say every age has its avatara. At the present time there is a
very famous miracle worker in South India called Satya Sai
Baba. He performs miracles almost every day which have
been witnessed by many people. Some say he is the avatara of
the Twentieth Century. He claims to be more than the Buddha, more than Jesus, more than Mohammed, but he is a
very ambiguous figure even in the eyes of many Hindus.

This is a good example of how a myth is created out of a
historical figure. But the avatara always belongs to cyclic
time. There is no finality. Each time righteousness declines

the avatara appears again on earth in some form or other. On the other hand, the whole point of the Christian Revelation was that Jesus came at the end of the age to bring all things to a completion: "It was His plan in the fullness of time to bring all things to a head in Christ, things in heaven and things on earth." There is a finality in this. This seems to me to be the distinctive character of the Incarnation. It is God's Revelation, not in mythical time, not as a recurrence from age to age, but in historic time among a historic people, at a historic time and place, in which all things are to be fulfilled. The death and resurrection of Christ is a unique event. In one sense it is a mythological event, an event of supreme symbolism. It is a sign of God's salvation for the whole creation and the whole of humanity. But it is a sign which is rooted in history. It is deeply significant that in the Apostles' Creed it is said that, "He was crucified under Pontius Pilate." He is placed in the centre of history. There were historians of the time, for example Suetonius, Tacitus, and Pliny, who actually mention Christ. This is a crucial point in history. God entered into historic time, into human existence as it is, and He suffered under Pontius Pilate. That is very difficult for the Hindu to understand. The Hindu ideal is to be above all suffering. I remember one Hindu Sannyasi telling me that he felt that Jesus wavered at the end, in the Garden of Gethsemane. He was overwhelmed by suffering. A Sannyasi would have been completely calm and free from all disturbance. Even on the cross Jesus cries out, "Why hast thou forsaken me?" and He feels abandoned by God. That is an imperfection for them.

When one looks at the Buddha, one sees that he is completely calm. He has passed beyond this world. But when we contemplate Jesus' suffering on the cross, we see how God has entered into humanity, into our human state, into human suffering and pain, into death. This is something quite different. Through that death and that resurrection we have the sign that God has entered into history, entered into this world, has redeemed history, and thereby has redeemed the world, has raised it up to new life beyond the world, beyond time, beyond space, to the final fulfillment.

So myth and history meet. My old tutor, C. S. Lewis, became a Christian because of his discovery of this relation between myth and history. From his childhood he was fascinated particularly by the Norse myths. When he was a young boy he experienced a sense of wonder in the myths of the Norsemen. They do not interest me at all, I am afraid, but he was fascinated by them. He steeped himself in these myths and at the same time he was more or less an agnostic, almost atheistic, philosopher. So the myth appealed to one side of his nature and philosophy to another. And then he began through a friend to see how the myth was present in the New Testament, in Christ, the Son of God, who becomes man, who dies and rises again. All this sounds like a myth, but that myth is present in a historic person, a historic place, a historic time. He realised that this is another kind of revelation, God's revelation in historic time and place, God entering into human history.

That aspect changes one's whole attitude to the world, and it changes one's attitude to material things. The Hindu is always in danger of dismissing matter as *maya*. The two words are actually linked, the root *ma* meaning to measure, so that maya is properly matter, that which is measured. But since matter is always changing, it is seen as the principle of change and becoming, and hence of mere appearance. The body is conceived as an appearance: you take on the appearance of a body, but you will lose that. All this world is passing away, and only the spirit will remain. The idea that the body itself is to be transformed, as the body of Jesus was transformed in the resurrection, and that the material universe is also to be transformed — that there is to be a "new creation" — this is something unique in the Biblical Revelation. The divine life penetrates history, time, suffering, and death, and then raises history and time and suffering and death into a new creation, a new order of being in which these things are not lost, not destroyed, but transfigured. This gives a value to every human person. With the doctrine of karma human persons get mixed up: you may have been Cleopatra in a past life, or somebody else. You are not yourself any longer, and in the end everything merges into one. You will enjoy the absolute bliss of the one. But "you" are really no longer there.

In the Christian view, each individual person, body and soul, has a unique character, is a unique image of God, and that person will not dissolve. The more universal you become, the more deeply personal you become. You do not diffuse yourself, you do not lose yourself as you grow in knowledge and understanding and love — you extend. You do not cease to be a person. You become more deeply personal. Jesus is the most personal being in history, and yet He is the most universal.

The Hindu always tends to think that when you reach the Beyond all your differences, body and soul, disappear, and you experience only the Divine Bliss, the *Sat Chit Ananda* — Being, Knowledge, and Bliss. But in the Christian view the whole meaning and purpose of creation was that God should reflect Himself in you, in me, in others, and in everything. The whole creation is not to disappear, but to be re-created and transfigured, to participate in the Divine Life, fulfilling itself in the Divine Bliss, the Divine Glory.

This brings a new perspective into our understanding of religion. The suffering of Christ and the death of Christ has a universal meaning. It is true that Rama and Krishna also have a universal meaning, just as Buddha's Enlightenment has a

The Cosmic Revelation

meaning for all humanity. But the life and death and resurrection of Christ have not only a meaning for all, but also an effect on history. Through the death and resurrection of Christ the history of man has been changed. Mankind has been changed because mankind is ultimately one, an organic, interdependent whole extending through space and time. The death and resurrection of Christ extends to all humanity, both in the past and in the present and in the future. In that sense it is a mythical event. It is a symbolic event and yet it is also a historic event. Here history has assumed universal meaning. The whole creation and the whole of humanity find an ultimate meaning, an ultimate purpose, in that death, resurrection, ascension, and final glorification. All this is to be found in St Paul in his conception of the "mystical body" of Christ, which is the "fullness of him who fills all in all." St Paul was faced with the beginnings of Gnosticism, particularly in Ephesus and the region of Asia Minor, where many currents of Oriental religion were present, and in confrontation with their teaching he was able to present Christ as the fulfillment of the whole cosmic and historic process.

Finally, what conclusion can we draw from this? The principle of complementarity. The danger of Christianity today is that it over-emphasises the importance of matter and science and history and human progress in this world striving for a better world. All these things have their value, of course, but the danger is that they absorb all our energies and all our attention. Yet we know that all is going to lead in the end to death. Death is the end of everything, unless there is a resurrection. And so the modern Christian view needs to be complemented with the constant awareness which the Hindu has of the eternal dimension of being.

In the same way, when we look on the external world we have to recognise that it is not just something for science to examine, to manipulate, to change and develop. It is a revelation of God. And that is something we have to recover. The whole creation is a sacrament, a revelation of God.

Then again, as regards human history, there is a process of development. We should be working for a better world. But if we think we are going to reach that goal in this world we will be frustrated and disappointed. We need to look beyond to the resurrection, and only then will that final fulfillment, justice, and truth be discovered.

So the world today needs what the Hindu can give of a sense of the sacramentality of the whole creation and of a transcendent world beyond time, beyond space, beyond this world altogether. This leads us to the point of understanding the sacramental character not only of this world but also of the Church. The Church also is a sacrament, a sacrament of Christ. And sacraments are signs. In the understanding of theology, a *sacramentum* is a sign, and sometimes that has been lost sight of, and there has been an over-realistic view of a sacrament. But a sacrament always remains a revelation of God under a sign. This was beautifully expressed in that hymn of St Thomas Aquinas *Adore te devote latens deitas.* The last verse of it goes:

> *"Jesu quem velatum nunc aspicio*
> *Oro fiat illud quod tam sitio*
> *Ut te revelata cernens facie*
> *Visu sim beatus tuae gloriae."*

The translation which really does not do justice to the beauty of the Latin is: "Jesus whom I now see under a veil, grant that that may be which I so much desire, that I may see Thee with face unveiled, and be blessed with the sight of Thy Glory."

We pray that the veil may be taken away, the veil of the sacrament, so that the reality may appear. In the humanity of Christ, God comes to us in a human being who suffers and dies and makes Himself known to us as a man, shares our very life with us and yet wants to take us beyond. Jesus, the humanity of Jesus, is a sacrament of God. It is a sign of God's grace, God's love, God's salvation, but we have to go beyond the sign to the reality, to the mystery of the Trinity. That is the last point I want to make.

In the Hindu Revelation the ultimate reality is *Sat Chit Ananda* — Being, Knowledge, Bliss. The search is for that ultimate Being, that 'ultimate reality' — *sat*, and that ultimate Being and Reality is Conscious; it is *chit*, 'consciousness,' a conscious awareness of infinite eternal being. And the consciousness of that eternal being is bliss, *ananda*, 'pure joy.' That is the goal of Hinduism — to reach that *sat-chit-ananda*, and that sat-chit-ananda is pure oneness, one without a second.

In the gospel there is a further depth revealed. In the ultimate reality there is revealed not merely an identity, but a communion. The final Christian Revelation is that the Godhead itself, the ultimate reality, is a communion of persons, a communion of persons in love, and that gives a further dimension to our understanding of reality. The Hindu believes that God is love in a sense, and that you can love God but not that the Godhead Itself is love. There cannot be love without two. If God is a pure monad as He is in Islam, as He tends to be in Hinduism, He cannot be love in Himself. But in the Christian concept the Godhead Itself is love, is a communion of love. There is a distinction within the Godhead Itself, distinction beyond our comprehension which we crudely express in terms of person and relation. These are human terms pointing to the reality. The reality is that God is love, that there is something which corresponds to personal communion in love in the Godhead, and we are called to share in that communion of love.

So also, in the mystical body of Christ which embraces all

redeemed humanity, we do not disappear in the Godhead, but we discover a personal relationship of love. Each person is fulfilled and is open to the other person; it is an inter-communion of love in which each embraces the other and all are embraced in God.

In the *Paradiso* in Dante's *Divine Comedy* there is a poetic description which goes as far as human intelligence can towards depicting this mystery of the Trinity as love. And that is what we are called to experience — this communion of love in the mystical body of Christ which embraces the whole creation. All the beauty of the creation is present there for our joy and our thanksgiving. The whole of redeemed humanity is there, and each of us, according to his capacity, is able to go out in love to others and to be embraced in love by others. All creation and all humanity are taken up into this infinite, incomprehensible, inexpressible Being of God, in whom — though we can never understand or comprehend Him — we know that there is this communion of charity, this communion of love. Jesus expresses it marvellously in the Gospel of St John, when He prays, "That they may be one. As Thou, Father in me and I in Thee, that they may be one in us." That is Christian *advaita*. We are one with one another and one with Christ; we are one in this mystery of the Godhead, and I do not think we can go beyond that. This would be an example of how to relate the Cosmic Revelation to the Christian Revelation. We are all engaged in this task, and it is not something fully accomplished; it is that to which we are moving.

GLOSSARY OF TERMS

abhaya mudra	gesture of fearlessness
Adam	Man (Hebrew)
Advaita	non-duality
Agni	fire
aham Brahmasmi	I am Brahman
amritam	immortality
anisa	without power
ananda	pure joy, bliss
apauruseya	without human authorship
aranya	forest
Aranyakas	Forest Books
arati	waving of lights and incense
asat	unreal
ashram	abode of ascetics, place of spiritual work
Atman	God within each person, Spirit
Atmavidya	knowledge of the Self
Avatara	incarnation, "descent"
avidya	ignorance
avyakta	unmanifest
Brahmā	Name of God, the Creator
Brahmachari	moving in Brahman, a student
Brahman	the Absolute, God
Brahmavidya	knowledge of God
bhakti	devotion
bhakti marga	the way of devotion

darshanas	philosophies
devas	shining ones, gods
Devatmasakti	the power of the Self of God
dharma	the law of life
Dios Pater	Father in Heaven (Greek)
Dvaita	duality
dyaus	sky
Dyaus Pita	Sky Father
Ekam eva advitya	One only without a second
Ekam sat	One Being
Ekam sat vipra bahuda vadanti	The One Being the wise call by many names
El Elyon	The Most High God (Hebrew)
Elohim	God, (plural – gods) (Hebrew)
Ganesh	elephant-headed God
garbha griha	house of the womb, inner sanctuary
Intellectus	the pure intelligence (Latin)
Isa	the Lord, power
Ithihasas	Epics
jivatman	individual soul
jnana marga	the way of knowledge
jyoti	light
karma	action, work
karmamarga	the way of work
Mahat	the Great Self
mantra	prayer or sacred word
maya	creative power, magic, illusion

mrityam	death
mulasthaman	inner sanctuary
neti, neti	not this, not this
Nirguna Brahman	God without attributes
nitya	eternal
Om	the sacred syllable, symbol of Brahman, the creative word
Parabrahman	the Supreme Spirit
Paramatman	,,
photismos	illumination (Greek)
pita	father
pleroma	fullness (Latin)
Pneuma	Spirit. see also Atman (Greek)
priya	dear
puja	sacrifice
pujari	priest
purnam	fullness
Puranas	mythological stories
Purusha	Cosmic Man, Cosmic Person
Purushottaman	The Supreme Person
ratio	lower reasoning mind (Latin)
Ric	hymn
rishis	seers
rita	the order of nature
Saguna Brahman	God with attributes
samatva	sameness
samsara	the wheel of life
Sanatana dharma	Eternal Religion
sannyasa	renunciation

sannyasi	a monk
Sarvam Khalvidam	All this world is Brahman
Brahman asti	
Sat	being
Sat cit ananda	Being, Consciousness, Bless
satya	truth
Shakti	the power of God
shanti	peace
Shantivanam	grove of peace
Siva	Name of God, the Destroyer and Regenerator
sloka	verse
Spiritus	spirit (Latin)
Tao	the order of Heaven (Chinese)
tapas	self control, penance
Tat	"That" in reference to God
Tat tvam asi	"Thou art That"
Veda	knowledge, sacred scripture
Vedanta	the end of the Vedas, philosophy
Vishnu	Name of God, the Preserver
Visishtadvaita	qualified non-duality
Yama	death